OECD/G20 Base Erosion and Profit Shifting Project

Mandatory Disclosure Rules, Action 12 - 2015 Final Report

Please cite this publication as:
OECD (2015), *Mandatory Disclosure Rules, Action 12 - 2015 Final Report*, OECD/G20 Base Erosion and Profit Shifting Project, OECD Publishing, Paris.
http://dx.doi.org/10.1787/9789264241442-en

ISBN 978-92-64-24137-4 (print)
ISBN 978-92-64-24144-2 (PDF)

Series: OECD/G20 Base Erosion and Profit Shifting Project
ISSN 2313-2604 (print)
ISSN 2313-2612 (online)

Photo credits: Cover © ninog – Fotolia.com

Corrigenda to OECD publications may be found on line at: *www.oecd.org/about/publishing/corrigenda.htm*.

Foreword

International tax issues have never been as high on the political agenda as they are today. The integration of national economies and markets has increased substantially in recent years, putting a strain on the international tax rules, which were designed more than a century ago. Weaknesses in the current rules create opportunities for base erosion and profit shifting (BEPS), requiring bold moves by policy makers to restore confidence in the system and ensure that profits are taxed where economic activities take place and value is created.

Following the release of the report *Addressing Base Erosion and Profit Shifting* in February 2013, OECD and G20 countries adopted a 15-point Action Plan to address BEPS in September 2013. The Action Plan identified 15 actions along three key pillars: introducing coherence in the domestic rules that affect cross-border activities, reinforcing substance requirements in the existing international standards, and improving transparency as well as certainty.

Since then, all G20 and OECD countries have worked on an equal footing and the European Commission also provided its views throughout the BEPS project. Developing countries have been engaged extensively via a number of different mechanisms, including direct participation in the Committee on Fiscal Affairs. In addition, regional tax organisations such as the African Tax Administration Forum, the *Centre de rencontre des administrations fiscales* and the *Centro Interamericano de Administraciones Tributarias*, joined international organisations such as the International Monetary Fund, the World Bank and the United Nations, in contributing to the work. Stakeholders have been consulted at length: in total, the BEPS project received more than 1 400 submissions from industry, advisers, NGOs and academics. Fourteen public consultations were held, streamed live on line, as were webcasts where the OECD Secretariat periodically updated the public and answered questions.

After two years of work, the 15 actions have now been completed. All the different outputs, including those delivered in an interim form in 2014, have been consolidated into a comprehensive package. The BEPS package of measures represents the first substantial renovation of the international tax rules in almost a century. Once the new measures become applicable, it is expected that profits will be reported where the economic activities that generate them are carried out and where value is created. BEPS planning strategies that rely on outdated rules or on poorly co-ordinated domestic measures will be rendered ineffective.

Implementation therefore becomes key at this stage. The BEPS package is designed to be implemented via changes in domestic law and practices, and via treaty provisions, with negotiations for a multilateral instrument under way and expected to be finalised in 2016. OECD and G20 countries have also agreed to continue to work together to ensure a consistent and co-ordinated implementation of the BEPS recommendations. Globalisation requires that global solutions and a global dialogue be established which go beyond OECD and G20 countries. To further this objective, in 2016 OECD and G20 countries will conceive an inclusive framework for monitoring, with all interested countries participating on an equal footing.

A better understanding of how the BEPS recommendations are implemented in practice could reduce misunderstandings and disputes between governments. Greater focus on implementation and tax administration should therefore be mutually beneficial to governments and business. Proposed improvements to data and analysis will help support ongoing evaluation of the quantitative impact of BEPS, as well as evaluating the impact of the countermeasures developed under the BEPS Project.

Table of contents

Figures

Table

Boxes

Abbreviations and acronyms

ATP	Aggressive Tax Planning
BEPS	Base Erosion and Profit Shifting
CAD	Canadian Dollar
CFA	Committee on Fiscal Affairs
CRA	Canada Revenue Agency
DD	Double Deduction
D/NI	Deduction/No Inclusion
DOTAS	Disclosure of Tax Avoidance Schemes (UK Legislation)
EUR	Euro
FTA	Forum on Tax Administration
GAAR	General Anti-Avoidance Rule
GBP	Great Britain Pound
HMRC	HM Revenue and Customs (United Kingdom)
IRC	Internal Revenue Code (United States)
IRS	Internal Revenue Service
JITSIC	Joint International Tax Shelter Information and Collaboration Network
MDR	Mandatory Disclosure Rules
MNE	Multinational Enterprise
OECD	Organisation for Economic Co-operation and Development
OTSA	Office of Tax Shelter Analysis
RTAT	Reporting of Tax Avoidance Transactions
SARS	South African Revenue Service
SEC	Securities and Exchange Commission
SPOC	Single Point of Contact
SRN	Scheme Reference Number
TOI	Transaction of Interest
TS	Tax Shelter
UK	United Kingdom

US	United States of America
USD	United States Dollar
VAT	Value Added Tax
WP11	Working Party No.11 on Aggressive Tax Planning
ZAR	South African Rand

Executive summary

The lack of timely, comprehensive and relevant information on aggressive tax planning strategies is one of the main challenges faced by tax authorities worldwide. Early access to such information provides the opportunity to quickly respond to tax risks through informed risk assessment, audits, or changes to legislation or regulations. Action 12 of the *Action Plan on Base Erosion and Profit Shifting* (BEPS Action Plan, OECD, 2013) recognised the benefits of tools designed to increase the information flow on tax risks to tax administrations and tax policy makers. It therefore called for recommendations regarding the design of mandatory disclosure rules for aggressive or abusive transactions, arrangements, or structures taking into consideration the administrative costs for tax administrations and businesses and drawing on experiences of the increasing number of countries that have such rules.

This Report provides a modular framework that enables countries without mandatory disclosure rules to design a regime that fits their need to obtain early information on potentially aggressive or abusive tax planning schemes and their users. The recommendations in this Report do not represent a minimum standard and countries are free to choose whether or not to introduce mandatory disclosure regimes. Where a country wishes to adopt mandatory disclosure rules, the recommendations provide the necessary flexibility to balance a country's need for better and more timely information with the compliance burdens for taxpayers. The Report also sets out specific recommendations for rules targeting international tax schemes, as well as for the development and implementation of more effective information exchange and co-operation between tax administrations.

Design principles and key objectives of a mandatory disclosure regime

Mandatory disclosure regimes should be clear and easy to understand, should balance additional compliance costs to taxpayers with the benefits obtained by the tax administration, should be effective in achieving their objectives, should accurately identify the schemes to be disclosed, should be flexible and dynamic enough to allow the tax administration to adjust the system to respond to new risks (or carve-out obsolete risks), and should ensure that information collected is used effectively.

The main objective of mandatory disclosure regimes is to increase transparency by providing the tax administration with early information regarding potentially aggressive or abusive tax planning schemes and to identify the promoters and users of those schemes. Another objective of mandatory disclosure regimes is deterrence: taxpayers may think twice about entering into a scheme if it has to be disclosed. Pressure is also placed on the tax avoidance market as promoters and users only have a limited opportunity to implement schemes before they are closed down.

Mandatory disclosure regimes both complement and differ from other types of reporting and disclosure obligations, such as co-operative compliance programmes, in that they are specifically designed to detect tax planning schemes that exploit vulnerabilities in the tax system, while also providing tax administrations with the flexibility to choose thresholds, hallmarks and filters to target transactions of particular interest and perceived areas of risk.

Key design features of a mandatory disclosure regime

In order to successfully design an effective mandatory disclosure regime, the following features need to be considered: who reports, what information to report, when the information has to be reported, and the consequences of non-reporting. In relation to the above design features, the Report recommends that countries introducing mandatory disclosure regimes:

- impose a disclosure obligation on both the promoter and the taxpayer, or impose the primary obligation to disclose on either the promoter or the taxpayer;
- include a mixture of specific and generic hallmarks, the existence of each of them triggering a requirement for disclosure. Generic hallmarks target features that are common to promoted schemes, such as the requirement for confidentiality or the payment of a premium fee. Specific hallmarks target particular areas of concern such as losses;
- establish a mechanism to track disclosures and link disclosures made by promoters and clients as identifying scheme users is also an essential part of any mandatory disclosure regime. Existing regimes identify these through the use of scheme reference numbers and/or by obliging the promoter to provide a list of clients. Where a country places the primary reporting obligation on a promoter, it is recommended that they also introduce scheme reference numbers and require, where domestic law allows, the production of client lists;
- link the timeframe for disclosure to the scheme being made available to taxpayers when the obligation to disclose is imposed on the promoter; link it to the implementation of the scheme when the obligation to disclose is imposed on the taxpayer;
- introduce penalties (including non-monetary penalties) to ensure compliance with mandatory disclosure regimes that are consistent with their general domestic law.

Coverage of international tax schemes

There are a number of differences between domestic and cross-border schemes that make the latter more difficult to target with mandatory disclosure regimes. International schemes are more likely to be specifically designed for a particular taxpayer or transaction and may involve multiple parties and tax benefits in different jurisdictions, which can make these schemes more difficult to target with domestic hallmarks. In order to overcome these difficulties, the Report recommends that:

- Countries develop hallmarks that focus on the type of cross-border BEPS outcomes that cause them concern. An arrangement or scheme that incorporates such a cross-border outcome would only be required to be disclosed, however, if that arrangement includes a transaction with a domestic taxpayer that has material tax consequences in the reporting country and the domestic taxpayer was aware or ought to have been aware of the cross-border outcome.

- Taxpayers that enter into intra-group transactions with material tax consequences are obliged to make reasonable enquiries as to whether the transaction forms part of an arrangement that includes a cross-border outcome that is specifically identified as reportable under their home jurisdictions' mandatory disclosure regime.

The application of these recommendations is illustrated in the Report with an example dealing with an imported hybrid mismatch arrangement of the type covered in the 2015 OECD/G20 BEPS report *Neutralising the Effects of Hybrid Mismatch Arrangements* (OECD, 2015).

Enhancing information sharing

Transparency is one of the three pillars of the OECD/G20 BEPS Project and a number of measures developed in the course of the Project will give rise to additional information being shared with, or between, tax administrations. The expanded Joint International Tax Shelter Information and Collaboration Network (JITSIC Network) of the OECD Forum on Tax Administration provides an international platform for an enhanced co-operation and collaboration between tax administrations, based on existing legal instruments, which could include co-operation on information obtained by participating countries under mandatory disclosure regimes.

Introduction

1. Governments need timely access to relevant information in order to identify and respond to tax risks posed by tax planning schemes. Access to the right information at an early stage allows tax administrations to improve the speed and accuracy of their risk assessment over a simple reliance on voluntary compliance and audit. At the same time, early identification of taxpayer compliance issues also gives tax authorities more flexibility in responding to tax risk and allows tax policy officials to make timely and informed decisions on appropriate legislative or regulatory responses to protect tax revenues.

2. A number of countries have therefore introduced disclosure initiatives to give them timely information about taxpayer behaviour and to facilitate the early identification of emerging policy issues. These initiatives include: rulings, penalty reductions for voluntary disclosure and the use of co-operative compliance programmes and additional reporting obligations as well as mandatory disclosure regimes. The objective of these initiatives is to either require or incentivise taxpayers and their advisers to provide tax authorities with relevant information about taxpayer compliance that is more detailed and timely than the information recorded on a tax return.

3. Mandatory disclosure regimes differ from these other disclosure and compliance initiatives in that they are specifically designed to require taxpayers and promoters to provide tax administrations with early disclosure of potentially aggressive or abusive tax planning arrangements if they fall within the definition of a *reportable scheme* set out under that regime. Mandatory disclosure therefore has a number of advantages when compared to other forms of disclosure initiative and allows tax administrations to obtain information much earlier in the tax compliance process (in certain cases before the structures have even been implemented). This can enable an accelerated response (statutory, administrative or regulatory) to transactions that are considered to be tax avoidance.

4. Mandatory disclosure regimes also provide the flexibility of a modular approach that allows tax administrations to select hallmarks and to apply thresholds and filters in order to focus the disclosure obligation on particular areas of perceived risk. The modular elements of the regime can be customised to fit with existing disclosure and compliance rules; to accommodate changing tax policy priorities and to minimise the compliance burden on taxpayers.

Action 12

5. The BEPS Action Plan recognises that one of the key challenges faced by tax authorities is a lack of timely, comprehensive and relevant information on potentially aggressive or abusive tax planning strategies. The *Action Plan on Base Erosion and Profit Shifting* (BEPS Action Plan, OECD, 2013a) notes that the availability of such information is essential to enable governments to quickly identify areas of tax policy and revenue

risk. While audits remain a key source of information on tax planning, they suffer from a number of constraints as tools for the early detection of tax planning schemes. Action 12 notes the usefulness of disclosure initiatives in addressing these issues and calls on OECD and G20 member countries to:

> Develop recommendations regarding the design of mandatory disclosure rules for aggressive or abusive transactions, arrangements, or structures, taking into consideration the administrative costs for tax administrations and businesses and drawing on experiences of the increasing number of countries that have such rules. The work will use a modular design allowing for maximum consistency but allowing for country specific needs and risks. One focus will be international tax schemes, where the work will explore using a wide definition of "tax benefit" in order to capture such transactions. The work will be co-ordinated with the work on co-operative compliance. It will also involve designing and putting in place enhanced models of information sharing for international tax schemes between tax administration (OECD, 2013a).

6. Action 12 therefore identifies three key outputs:

- recommendations for the modular design of mandatory disclosure rules;
- a focus on international tax schemes and consideration of a wide definition of tax benefit to capture relevant transactions;
- designing and putting in place enhanced models of information sharing for international tax schemes.

7. Action 12 provides that the recommendations for the design of mandatory disclosure rules should allow maximum consistency between countries while being sensitive to country specific needs and risks and the costs for tax administrations and business. The design recommendations should also take into account the role played by other compliance and disclosure initiatives such as co-operative compliance.

Work to date on this issue

8. The OECD issued a report on transparency and disclosure initiatives in 2011 (*Tackling Aggressive Tax Planning through Improved Transparency and Disclosure*, OECD, 2011). The 2011 Report explained the importance of timely, targeted and comprehensive information to counter aggressive tax planning; provided an overview of disclosure initiatives introduced in certain OECD countries (including mandatory disclosure) and discussed those countries' experiences regarding such initiatives. The 2011 Report recommended countries review the disclosure initiatives outlined in the report "with a view to evaluating the introduction of those best suited to their particular needs and circumstances."

9. In 2013 the OECD issued a report on co-operative compliance programmes (*Co-operative Compliance: A Framework: From Enhanced Relationship to Co-Operative Compliance*, OECD, 2013b). This 2013 Report (OECD, 2013b) was a follow-up to a 2008 *Study on the Role of Tax Intermediaries* (OECD, 2008), which encouraged tax authorities to establish enhanced relationships with their large business taxpayers. Under co-operative compliance programmes, taxpayers agree to make full disclosure of material tax issues and transactions they have undertaken to enable tax authorities to understand their tax impact. Co-operative compliance relationships allow for a joint approach to tax risk management and compliance and can result in more effective risk assessment and better use of resources by the tax administration. The 2013 Report (OECD, 2013b) noted the number of countries

that had developed co-operative compliance programmes since the publication of the 2008 Study and concluded that the value of such programmes was now well-established.

10. Both mandatory disclosure and co-operative compliance are intended to improve transparency, risk assessment and ultimately taxpayer compliance. They do this is in different ways and may be aimed at different taxpayer populations, for instance co-operative compliance programmes often focus on the largest corporate taxpayers. However, as mentioned later in this report, mandatory disclosure can reinforce the effectiveness of a co-operative compliance regime by ensuring that there is a level playing field in terms of the disclosure and tax transparency required from all taxpayers.

What this report covers

11. This report provides an overview of mandatory disclosure regimes, based on the experiences of countries that have such regimes, and sets out recommendations for a modular design of a mandatory disclosure regime. The recommended design utilises a standard framework to ensure maximum consistency while preserving sufficient flexibility to allow tax administrations to control the quantity and type of disclosure. This report also sets out recommendations for a mandatory disclosure regime designed to capture international tax schemes. The report is divided into four chapters:

- Chapter 1 provides an overview of the key features of a mandatory disclosure regime and considers its interaction with other disclosure initiatives and compliance tools.
- Chapter 2 sets out both the framework and features for the modular design of a mandatory disclosure regime.
- Chapter 3 looks at international transactions and considers how these could best be captured by a mandatory disclosure regime.
- Chapter 4 considers exchange of information in the context of international schemes.

Bibliography

OECD (2013a), *Action Plan on Base Erosion and Profit Shifting*, OECD, Paris, http://dx.doi.org/10.1787/9789264202719-en.

OECD (2013b), *Co-operative Compliance: A Framework: From Enhanced Relationship to Co-operative Compliance*, OECD, Paris, http://dx.doi.org/10.1787/9789264200852-en.

OECD (2011), *Tackling Aggressive Tax Planning through Improved Transparency and Disclosure*, OECD, Paris, www.oecd.org/ctp/exchange-of-tax-information/48322860.pdf.

OECD (2008), *Study into the Role of Tax Intermediaries*, OECD, Paris, http://dx.doi.org/10.1787/9789264041813-en.

Chapter 1

Overview of mandatory disclosure

Objectives

12. The main purpose of mandatory disclosure rules is to provide early information regarding potentially aggressive or abusive tax planning schemes and to identify the promoters[1] and users of those schemes. Early detection from obtaining quick and relevant information enhances tax authorities' effectiveness in their compliance activities. As a result, some of the resources that would otherwise be dedicated to detecting tax avoidance, for example through audit, can be redeployed to review and respond to scheme disclosures. In addition early information can enable tax administrations to quickly respond to changes in taxpayer behaviour through operational policy, legislative or regulatory changes.

13. Another objective of mandatory disclosure rules is deterrence. A reduction in the promotion and use of tax avoidance can be achieved by altering the economics of tax avoidance. Taxpayers may think twice about entering into a scheme if it has to be disclosed and they know that the tax authorities may take a different position on the tax consequences of that scheme or arrangement.

14. Mandatory disclosure rules also place pressure on the tax avoidance market as promoters and users only have a limited opportunity to implement schemes before they are closed down. In order to enhance the effect of a disclosure regime it is therefore important that countries' tax administration and legislative systems can react rapidly to close down opportunities for tax avoidance.

15. Whilst countries have reported some different experiences with respect to the deterrence effect, the objectives of existing different mandatory disclosure rules can be summarised as follows:

- to obtain early information about potentially aggressive or abusive tax avoidance schemes in order to inform risk assessment;
- to identify schemes, and the users and promoters of schemes in a timely manner;
- to act as a deterrent, to reduce the promotion and use of avoidance schemes.

16. A discussion of the effectiveness of mandatory disclosure in achieving these objectives is set out below.

Basic elements of mandatory disclosure

17. In order to achieve the objectives set out above, mandatory disclosure regimes have to address a number of basic design questions which determine their scope and application as follows:

- **Who has to report:** Mandatory disclosure rules can require disclosure from taxpayers (the users) and/or planners (promoters or advisors) of potential avoidance schemes.
- **What has to be reported:** This can be broken down into two different questions:
  - Countries first need to decide what types of schemes and arrangements should be disclosed under the regime (i.e. the definition of what is a "reportable scheme"). As noted later in this report, the fact that a scheme is reportable does not automatically mean that it involves tax avoidance. Some of the hallmarks described herein have generally been linked to abusive tax transactions, but may also be found in legitimate transactions. In addition it is unlikely that

a disclosure regime will be designed to pick up all tax avoidance, instead disclosure is likely to be targeted on the areas of avoidance and aggressive tax planning that are perceived to give rise to the greatest risks.

- Countries also need to determine what information needs to be disclosed about a reportable scheme. This involves striking a balance between ensuring the information is clear and useful and avoiding undue compliance burdens for taxpayers.

- **When information is reported:** The purpose of mandatory disclosure rules is to provide the tax administration with early information on certain tax planning schemes and their users. The determination of when promoters and/or users are required to make a disclosure is therefore key to achieving that goal.
- **What other obligations (if any) should be placed on promoters and/or scheme users:** For instance countries might require users of schemes to report a unique identification number on their return in order to identify users of disclosed schemes. Disclosure rules can also require promoters to provide clients lists to the tax administration.
- **What are the consequences of non-compliance:** Non-compliance with disclosure rules generally triggers penalties. In addition, countries may apply other sanctions to enforce mandatory disclosure rules and deter non-compliance.
- **What are the consequences of disclosure:** Mandatory disclosure regimes need to be clear about the consequences of disclosure for the taxpayer and advisor. In particular countries should make it clear that reporting a scheme does not mean that the scheme is accepted by the tax administration or that it will not be challenged.
- **How to use the information collected:** Mandatory disclosure regimes should provide relevant information about tax avoidance schemes so, in addition to defining the scope of the rules as mentioned above, countries need to consider how to make full use of the information collected in order to improve compliance.

Design principles

18. The specific approach taken to introducing mandatory disclosure rules will vary from country to country. Nevertheless, the text below considers the key design principles.

Mandatory disclosure rules should be clear and easy to understand

19. Mandatory disclosure rules should be drafted as clearly as possible to provide taxpayers with certainty about what is required by the regime. Lack of clarity and certainty can lead to inadvertent failure to disclose (and the imposition of penalties), which may increase resistance to such rules from taxpayers. Additionally, a lack of clarity could result in a tax administration receiving poor quality or irrelevant information.

Mandatory disclosure rules should balance additional compliance costs to taxpayers with the benefits obtained by the tax administration.

20. As mandatory disclosure rules impose an obligation to disclose certain transactions on taxpayers and/or promoters they will increase upfront compliance costs. Such rules, however, will provide tax administrations with better information on avoidance transactions

and should enable them to use their resources more efficiently. This better targeting, or improved risk assessment, could also bring benefits to taxpayers as enquiries will be focused on areas of real concern to the tax administration.

21. The scope and extent of any disclosure obligation is key in terms of achieving a balance. Unnecessary or additional requirements will increase taxpayer costs and may undermine a tax administration's ability to effectively use the data provided.

Mandatory disclosure rules should be effective in achieving the intended policy objectives and accurately identify relevant schemes

22. As mentioned above the key objective of a mandatory disclosure regime is to obtain early notification of avoidance schemes and their users and promoters. Any rules therefore need to be drafted so that they capture sufficient information on the schemes and arrangements a tax administration is concerned about. In addition they should provide information to enable identification of users and promoters. It is impractical for a mandatory disclosure regime to target all transactions that raise tax avoidance concerns and the identification of "hallmarks" is a key factor to setting the scope of the rules. However the hallmarks will need to reflect specific country needs or risks.

Information collected under mandatory disclosure should be used effectively

23. A tax administration needs to implement effective procedures for making best use of the information disclosed by taxpayers. This means setting up a process to review disclosures and identify the potential tax policy and revenue implications. Once issues have been identified, effective communication within the tax administration is necessary to ensure these issues are fully understood and addressed. While this may entail the commitment of additional resources, this cost could be offset by resource savings from quicker and more efficient identification of emerging tax policy and revenue issues.

Comparison with other disclosure initiatives

24. A number of countries operate information or compliance initiatives in addition to or instead of having a mandatory disclosure regime. The other types of disclosure initiatives used by tax administrations to collect taxpayer compliance information are described in further detail in the Report on *Tackling Aggressive Tax Planning through Improved Transparency and Disclosure* (2011 Report, OECD, 2011) and include:

- **Rulings regimes** that enable taxpayers to obtain a tax authority's view on how the tax law applies to a particular transaction or set of circumstances and provides taxpayers with some degree of certainty on the tax consequences. Rulings can, at least in part, play a similar role to disclosure regimes in that a taxpayer will typically apply for a ruling in anticipation of entering into a transaction. The usefulness of rulings regimes as a source of information on transactions involving tax avoidance may however be limited where the tax administration does not rule on transactions that involve abusive or aggressive tax planning schemes because taxpayers will have no incentive to apply for such rulings.
- **Additional reporting obligations** that require taxpayers to disclose particular transactions, investments or tax consequences usually as part of the return filing process.

- **Surveys and Questionnaires** that are used by some tax administrations to gather information from certain groups of taxpayers with a view to undertaking risk assessments.
- **Voluntary disclosure** as means of reducing taxpayer penalties.
- **Co-operative compliance programmes** where participating taxpayers agree to make full and true disclosure of material tax issues and transactions and provide sufficient information to understand the transaction and its tax impact.

A comparative summary of these information disclosure initiatives is set out in Table 1.1.

25. In each case, the objective of these disclosure initiatives is, to a greater or lesser extent, to require, or incentivise taxpayers and their advisers to provide tax authorities with relevant information on taxpayer behaviour that is either more detailed, or more timely, than the information recorded on a tax return. These other disclosure and compliance initiatives have different objectives to mandatory disclosure and are not exclusively focused on identifying the tax policy and revenue risks raised by aggressive tax planning. They therefore typically lack the broad scope of a mandatory disclosure regime (capturing any type of tax or taxpayer) or the focus on obtaining specific information about promoters, taxpayers and defined schemes. The key feature that distinguishes mandatory disclosure from these other types of reporting obligations is that mandatory disclosure regimes are specifically designed to detect tax planning schemes that exploit vulnerabilities in the tax system while also providing tax administrations with the flexibility to choose thresholds, hallmarks and filters in order to target transactions of particular interest and perceived areas of risk. A more detailed discussion of the key differences between mandatory disclosure regimes and other types of disclosure initiative is set out below.

Mandatory disclosure applies to a broader range of persons

26. Because mandatory disclosure regimes apply to all taxpayers (both large and small) and not simply those who choose to disclose through a voluntary compliance measure, they have a broad scope and can capture the largest possible set of taxpayers, tax types and transactions. Mandatory disclosure regimes also include third parties involved in the design, marketing, or implementation of tax planning schemes. In contrast to voluntary disclosure initiatives, which only incentivise a taxpayer to disclose details of their tax planning arrangements, mandatory disclosure is compulsory, so that any scheme targeted by the regime is required to be disclosed by all taxpayers and their advisers. Ruling regimes, for example, can provide tax administrations with useful information on transactions being undertaken by taxpayers and how taxpayers are interpreting and applying the law. However because rulings regimes are voluntary compliance initiatives, they will apply to a smaller number of self-selected taxpayers.

27. While an effective co-operative compliance programme or targeted questionnaires can provide a source of information on tax planning schemes, neither of these disclosure initiatives target the same range of taxpayers or the advisers and other third parties responsible for the design and implementation of such schemes. Although taxpayer surveys and questionnaires can reach a wider group of taxpayers than a co-operative compliance regime, they can only cover selected risks and the information obtained on those risks will depend on the design of the questionnaire. The effectiveness of questionnaires will also depend on the powers of the tax administration to require taxpayers to respond.

Mandatory disclosure provides specific information on the scheme, users and suppliers

28. Many countries impose reporting obligations on their taxpayers in relation to particular transactions or require taxpayers to specifically disclose the application of the particular regime. These additional reporting obligations enable tax authorities to improve audit efficiency through better data collection and analysis. However, in contrast to mandatory disclosure regimes, additional reporting obligations do not focus on tax avoidance and typically do not directly provide tax administrations with information on tax planning techniques.

29. In the absence of a mandatory disclosure regime, tax authorities can not only find it difficult to identify a scheme from available information but may also find that, by the time the scheme has been identified, it is too late to prevent significant revenue loss. It can also be difficult to identify all the users of a scheme, without using substantial additional tax administration resource, so that quantifying the tax loss, or designing an effective compliance strategy, can be challenging.

30. Because mandatory disclosure requires promoters and taxpayers to report specific scheme information directly to the tax administration it is a more efficient and effective method of obtaining comprehensive information on tax planning than relying on an analysis or audit of tax return information. Mandatory disclosure also provides tax administrations with information on the users of the scheme and those responsible for promoting and implementing it. This use of client lists and scheme identification numbers allows the tax administration to rapidly obtain an accurate picture of the extent of the tax risk posed by a scheme and to easily identify when a taxpayer has used a scheme. Access to client lists also opens up the possibility of using other tax compliance tools such as direct communication with taxpayers.

Mandatory disclosure provides information early in the tax compliance process

31. One of the key objectives of a mandatory disclosure regime is to provide tax administrations with early information on tax planning behaviour. Early warning allows tax administrations to respond more quickly to tax policy and revenue risks through operational, legislative or regulatory changes. Other disclosure initiatives do not generally provide tax administrations with the same degree of advanced warning. Ruling applications are perhaps the exception, in that taxpayers usually apply for a ruling in anticipation of undertaking a transaction. Rulings regimes, however, are voluntary disclosure initiatives used by a subsection of the taxpayer population and therefore do not provide tax administrations with a comprehensive overview of taxpayer behaviour or a reliable indicator of emerging tax policy and revenue risks.

Co-ordination with other disclosure and compliance tools

32. Both the decision as to whether to introduce a mandatory disclosure regime and the structure and content of such a regime depend on a number of factors including an assessment of the tax policy and revenue risks posed by tax planning within the jurisdiction and the availability of other disclosure and compliance tools. In particular, the additional intelligence on tax planning behaviour that a tax administration obtains under a mandatory disclosure regime will depend on the breadth and effectiveness of other information disclosure, such as co-operative compliance and rulings regimes, that collect substantially the same information. Nevertheless the analysis in this chapter suggests that mandatory

disclosure provides tax administrations with a number of advantages over other forms of disclosure initiative in that it requires both taxpayers and promoters to report information, early in the tax compliance process, on tax planning schemes that raise particular tax policy or revenue risks. Countries that have introduced mandatory disclosure rules indicate that they both deter aggressive tax planning behaviour and improve the quality, timeliness and efficiency in gathering information on tax planning schemes allowing for more effective compliance, legislative and regulatory responses. This is supported by the data set out in Table 1.1.

33. While other disclosure and compliance initiatives can also produce similar outcomes they do not fulfil exactly the same objectives because they: apply to a different and in some cases a potentially smaller population of taxpayers, promoters, advisors and intermediaries; do not target or provide the same level of information on avoidance or provide that information later in the tax compliance process.

34. Just as disclosure initiatives such as rulings and co-operative compliance programmes are not a good substitute for a mandatory disclosure regime, equally mandatory disclosure cannot replace or remove the need for these other type of disclosure and compliance tools. Mandatory disclosure can, however, reinforce other disclosure and tax compliance tools such as co-operative compliance or voluntary disclosure in ensuring a more level playing field as between large corporates and other taxpayers that do not have the same kind of compliance relationship with the tax administration. In deciding whether to introduce a mandatory disclosure regime or determining the kinds of arrangement targeted by the regime a tax administration will need to take account of other information gathering tools and its risk assessment processes so that they can be co-ordinated and harmonised as far as possible. For example, if a jurisdiction already has specific reporting rules on certain transactions it should consider whether to exclude these from the scope of any mandatory disclosure regime.[2] On the other hand a scheme that is required to be disclosed under a mandatory disclosure regime should not be required to be disclosed a second time under a voluntary disclosure requirement in order, for example, to benefit from a reduction in taxpayer penalties.

35. There is also some inevitable (and desirable) overlap between the operation and effects of mandatory disclosure and a General Anti-Avoidance Rule (GAAR). A GAAR provides tax administrations with an ability to respond directly to instances of tax avoidance that have been disclosed under a mandatory disclosure regime. Equally, from a deterrence perspective, a taxpayer is less likely to enter into a tax planning scheme knowing that the tax outcomes will need to be disclosed and may subsequently be challenged by the tax administration. Mandatory disclosure and GAARs are therefore mutually complementary from a compliance perspective. Equally, however, the purpose of a mandatory disclosure regime is to provide the tax administration with information on a wider range of tax policy and revenue risks other than those raised by transactions that would be classified as avoidance under a GAAR. Accordingly the definition of a "reportable scheme" for disclosure purposes will generally be broader than the definition of tax avoidance schemes covered by a GAAR and should also cover transactions that are perceived to be aggressive or high-risk from a tax planning perspective.

Effectiveness of mandatory disclosure[3]

36. Amongst the OECD and G20 countries, mandatory disclosure rules have been introduced in the United States, Canada, South Africa, the United Kingdom, Portugal, Ireland, Israel, and Korea.[4] In 1984, the United States first introduced such rules, which

Table 1.1. **Comparison of Mandatory Disclosure Rules (MDR) with other regimes**

	MDR	Rulings	Additional reporting obligation	Surveys	Penalty reductions for early disclosures	Co-operative compliance programmes
1. Who has reporting obligation under a regime						
Taxpayers	All taxpayers	All taxpayers	All taxpayers	Sub-set of taxpayers	All taxpayers	Sub-set of taxpayers
Third parties	Promoters	No	No	No	No	No
2. What has to be reported						
Type of transactions	Tax avoidance: Areas of known risks, and new or potentially abusive transactions	Not primarily designed to capture tax avoidance[a]	May not be targeted at avoidance schemes or only at specific schemes	Particular areas of known risk	Can apply to all tax avoidance and to evasion	Tax planning or tax avoidance undertaken by taxpayers within the programme
Information on promoter	Yes[b]	No	No	No	No	No
3. Effect						
Certainty for taxpayer	No	Yes, specific transactions	No	No	No	Yes
Deterrence on consumption side[c]	Yes	Yes	Yes	Yes	Yes	Yes
Deterrence on supply of avoidance	Yes	No	No	No	No	No
Timing	Can obtain information at early stage	Can obtain information at early stage	Generally part of return filing process, so no early detection	Timing variable – unlikely to provide early detection	Timing variable – limited early detection	Can obtain information at early stage
Nature of reporting requirement	Mandatory	Voluntary	Mandatory	Mandatory	Voluntary	Voluntary

Notes: a. Several countries expressed the opinion that their rulings regime did provide information on avoidance. This has not been tested but the comments made in the table and in this chapter relate to how rulings regimes are generally applied in the countries involved in this work.

b. Information on the promoter is obtained except in the very limited circumstances in which only taxpayers report.

c. While the extent of any deterrent effect is difficult to measure, MDR may have a stronger deterrent effect than other regimes because it particularly targets aggressive tax planning schemes and taxpayers can expect the disclosure to be scrutinised by tax authorities with a view to taking early action to address any tax policy or revenue risks.

were last revised significantly in 2004. Canada followed in 1989 with a Tax Shelter (TS) regime for a specific tax planning arrangement involving gifting arrangements and the acquisition of property. In addition, new mandatory Reporting of Tax Avoidance Transactions (RTAT) legislation with much broader reporting requirements was enacted in June 2013. South Africa introduced disclosure rules in 2003 and revised them in 2008. The United Kingdom enacted disclosure rules in 2004 and revised them substantially in 2006. Further substantial amendments entered into force on 1 January 2011. Portugal and Ireland introduced their mandatory disclosure regime in 2008 and 2011 respectively and since then Korea and Israel have also introduced mandatory disclosure rules. The design (and consequently the effect) of these regimes varies from one country to the next. In general, however, as noted above, the main objectives of mandatory disclosure rules can be summarised as follows:

- to obtain early information about tax avoidance schemes in order to inform risk assessment;
- to identify schemes, and the users and promoters of schemes in a timely manner;
- to act as a deterrent, to reduce the promotion and use of avoidance schemes.

37. Not all of the countries with mandatory disclosure regimes have collected data on the effectiveness of their regime in terms of these objectives. Much of the information in this section focuses on data and statistics provided by the United Kingdom along with some specific examples and data provided by other countries. However even though the available data is not comprehensive or detailed, the feedback from those with disclosure regimes provides a reasonably consistent picture that suggests that mandatory disclosure is successful in meeting its objectives.

Obtaining early information

38. By providing tax administrations with an effective "early warning" system for emerging tax policy and revenue risks, tax administrations have a wider range of options for addressing these risks through compliance, legislative or regulatory responses.

39. The UK Disclosure of Tax Avoidance Schemes (DOTAS) has provided early information about tax avoidance schemes, allowing the UK Government, where appropriate, to introduce legislation closing them down before significant tax was lost. 925 of the 2 366 avoidance schemes disclosed up to 2013 have been closed by legislation (one legislative change can close more than one scheme: over 200 stamp duty land tax schemes were closed by just 3 legislative changes). Schemes can also be shut down very quickly. For example, on one occasion, a scheme was closed down within a week of the disclosure, protecting millions in tax revenue.

40. The United Kingdom's experience has been that the early years following DOTAS being introduced gave rise to an initial spike of action to close down loopholes by making legislative change as more information became available about the schemes being promoted in the market.[5] This has tailed off since, for a number of reasons including:

- the gradual narrowing of the scope for successful avoidance scheme design by successive legislative change;
- some of the larger and more expert advisory firms moving out of the avoidance design market targeted by DOTAS;

- other tools being added to the counter avoidance toolkit, such as targeted anti-avoidance rules, GAAR, actions focused on promoters;
- a downshift in the expertise of the type of firm promoting avoidance schemes meaning that disclosed schemes can be challenged under existing law and do not require a legislative response.

41. Examples of how mandatory disclosure has informed legislative change are also available from other regimes. For instance a number of disclosures were received under the Irish mandatory disclosure regime in relation to employee benefit trusts.[6] A wide reaching anti-avoidance provision was introduced in Irish Finance Act 2013 which counteracted these schemes.

42. In South Africa any preference share that is redeemable within 10 years of issue is listed as a reportable arrangement. These arrangements make up the majority of transactions reported and the data collected has provided an insight into how preference share funding is utilised. This understanding has informed the design of the new hybrid equity tax rules that have been recently introduced.

Improved identification of schemes, users and promoters

43. The introduction of a mandatory disclosure regime should allow a tax administration to reduce their reliance on audit and data analysis as a mechanism for detecting tax avoidance.

44. The Aggressive Tax Planning (ATP) Directory is a secure database of tax planning schemes maintained by certain OECD and G20 countries. The Directory is populated by ATP schemes submitted by the countries that have access to it and it is used to identify tax planning trends and formulate detection and response strategies. Of the more than 400 schemes posted on the Directory, two-thirds have been identified through data analysis and audit. However the reliance on audit and data analysis would appear to be much lower for countries that have introduced mandatory disclosure regimes. If the same analysis is undertaken using a subset of four member countries with mandatory disclosure regimes,[7] the number of contributed schemes that the tax administration has identified through audit and data analysis falls to one-third with another one-third coming from mandatory disclosure. This would indicate that countries with mandatory disclosure regimes place significantly less reliance on audits and data analysis as a method of detecting tax planning schemes.

45. Looking at specific countries, the information provided by the UK DOTAS regime about the take up of a scheme has been useful in putting together an operational response. Client lists have also enabled the deployment of UK tax administration resources to be co-ordinated and planned more effectively because they identify the number of possible cases at an early stage. Client lists have also provided an additional mechanism for checking that schemes are disclosed by all users.

46. The UK tax administration has also used the opportunity created by early disclosure to intervene with promoters. For example, in one case it was evident that a scheme did not work and was based on an incorrect interpretation of the relevant tax law. As a result of talking to the promoter and issuing a communication to warn potential users, the promoter agreed not to market this scheme. This resulted in a more efficient use of resource compared to waiting for the scheme to be widely sold and then challenging individual returns.

47. Under the Canadian TS regime promoters are required to obtain an identification number before selling a scheme and promoters must report all participants and amounts by the end of February of the following year. This information enabled the Canada Revenue Agency (CRA) to more quickly determine the extent of the problems raised by tax shelters involving charitable donations. In addition, having the names of the participants up-front made it much easier to conduct audits and meant that time was not spent on having to identify participants. The CRA has now denied more than CAD 5.9 billion in donation claims and reassessed over 182 000 taxpayers who participated in these gifting tax shelters. In addition the CRA has revoked the charitable status of 47 charitable organisations that participated in these arrangements, and assessed third party penalties against promoters etc. to the extent of CAD 137 million.

Deterrence

48. Taxpayers are likely to adopt a more cautious approach before entering into a tax planning scheme if they know it has to be reported and that the tax authorities may take a different position on the tax consequences of that scheme or arrangement. Because mandatory disclosure regimes also require disclosure from third parties involved in the design and marketing of a scheme it targets both the demand and the supply-side of the tax avoidance market. Influencing the behaviour of promoters, advisers and intermediaries may reduce the incidence of aggressive tax planning more quickly and in a more cost-effective way than strategies that focus exclusively on the taxpayer. The fact that mandatory disclosure provides an early warning system for tax administrations also alters the economics for promoters as users may only have a limited opportunity to implement schemes before they are closed down. While the extent of any deterrent effect is difficult to measure the data and examples set out in Figures 1.1 and 1.2 suggest that there is such an effect.

49. Under the UK DOTAS, 2 366 avoidance schemes were disclosed up to 31 March 2013. However, the number of schemes disclosed annually has reduced over the years and most mainstream tax advisers have stopped promoting the marketed avoidance schemes caught by the disclosure rules, which is now largely the province of a small minority of tax advisory firms, generally referred to a "boutique" firms in the United Kingdom. DOTAS is believed to be one, but not the only, factor in this change in behaviour.

50. There has been a general decrease in the number of schemes disclosed over the years since DOTAS was introduced, which also implies the decrease in the number of reportable schemes which have been used. When DOTAS was first introduced a significant number of historic schemes were disclosed. As numbers have got much smaller in recent years, further reductions are naturally less pronounced, which the UK tax administration considers shows the market is shrinking, but they have put measures in place to check that this is not down to non-compliance with DOTAS.

51. As the UK regime has matured and the number of reportable schemes has reduced, the United Kingdom has looked to use the information provided by the regime to influence behaviour in additional ways. For instance, the UK tax authority may use information on disclosures and client lists to make early contact with promoters and potential users to encourage them to change their view of a scheme. Under legislation introduced in 2014, the United Kingdom may also require disputed tax in disclosed schemes to be paid before the dispute is settled, thus ensuring that the Exchequer, not the taxpayer, holds the benefit of the money during the dispute.

52. Similarly in the United States, the number of reports of all types of reportable transactions including listed transactions and transactions of interest has reduced in the

years since those concepts were introduced in 2000 and 2006, respectively. These reductions might be attributable to more than one cause, including trends in the overall economy. When a transaction is listed, however, the notice that the transaction is likely to be disallowed, the disclosure requirement, and imposition of penalties for failure to disclose generally create a chilling effect, and it becomes less likely that taxpayers will enter into substantially similar transactions. The same effect arose with the other reportable transaction categories when they were first added (e.g. contractual protection, confidentiality, etc.).

53. In Canada, one of the most common and pervasive schemes used to abuse the tax deductions and credits available for donations made to registered charities was gifting arrangement tax shelters. These arrangements became common in the early 2000s and reached their peak in 2006 with approximately 49 000 participants in that year. The sales and number of participants/investors for gifting tax shelters, for the period 2006-13 calendar years are illustrated in Figure 1.1.

Figure 1.1. **Gifting tax shelters – participants and donations (Canada, 2006-13)**

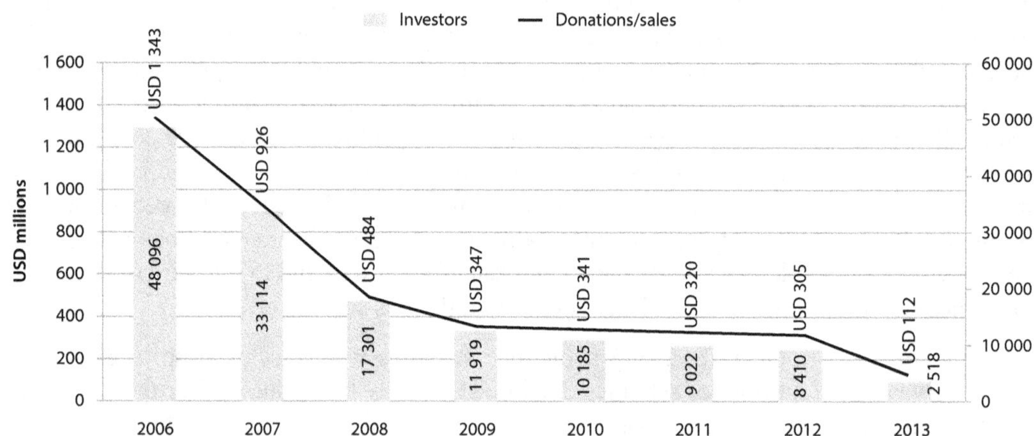

Figure 1.2. **Annual disclosure by hallmark type (South Africa, 2009-14)**

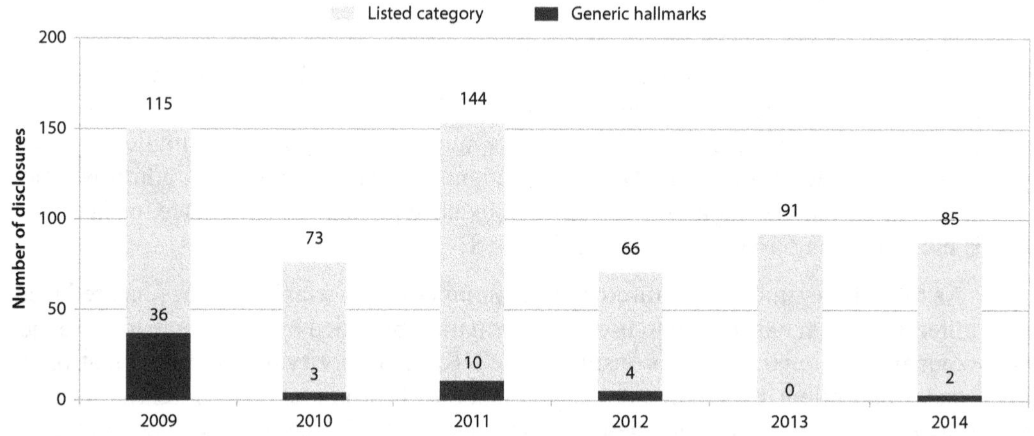

54. The South African reportable arrangements legislation came into force in 2005 and new legislation took effect in 2008. The new legislation enhanced the scope of reportable arrangements, in particular, the scope of the generic hallmarks. Under the South African

regime, 629 arrangements have been reported since 2009. In the majority of cases the disclosures have been made by several large companies. Whilst the data from South Africa presents a more mixed picture in terms of the deterrent effects Figure 1.2 indicates that the majority of reports under the generic hallmarks were made during 2009 and the number of arrangements disclosed annually under those hallmarks has reduced significantly. Since this data was collected South Africa has extended the scope of its mandatory disclosure regime with the addition of specific hallmarks targeting transactions that are of particular concern to the South African tax administration.

55. This chapter has set out the basic objectives and design principles of a mandatory disclosure regime, identifies the key features of mandatory disclosure which distinguish it from other types of disclosure initiative and describes the effectiveness of mandatory disclosure as a compliance tool based on data obtained from countries that have mandatory disclosure regimes. However the actual impact of mandatory disclosure, from a tax compliance perspective, will depend on the requirements imposed on taxpayers by the regime and whether the regime adheres to the design principles set out in this chapter.

Notes

1. The term "Promoters", as used in this report, is applied broadly to capture both those who promote a tax shelter or avoidance scheme in the traditional sense, and intermediaries (such as material advisors) who facilitate the implementation of a reportable scheme. See further *Study into the Role of Tax Intermediaries* (OECD, 2008).

2. For example, the United States no longer includes transactions with a significant book-tax difference in its mandatory disclosure regime after the issuance of a net income/loss reconciliation schedule which provides the detailed information on transactions with significant book-tax differences. See further paragraph 128.

3. This section was prepared on the basis of information on mandatory disclosure regimes provided by countries (Canada, Ireland, South Africa, the United Kingdom and the United States).

4. For relevant primary legislation in the US, see sections 6011, 6111, 6112, 6707, 6707A, 6662A, and 6708 of the Internal Revenue Code, as well as the Treasury regulations issued thereunder. In Canada, see sections 237.1, 237.3, 143.2 and 248 of the Income Tax Act and in South Africa, see sections 80M to 80T of the Income Tax Act. In the UK, see Finance Act 2004, Part 7(s. 306 to s. 319) and in Portugal, see Decree-Law No. 29/2008 of 25 February 2008. In Ireland, see section 149 of the Finance Act 2010.

5. A link to the UK tax avoidance disclosure statistics is here: www.gov.uk/government/uploads/system/uploads/attachment_data/file/379821/HMRC_-_Tax_avoidance_disclosure_statistics_1_Aug_2004_to_30_Sept_2014.pdf (accessed on 16 July 2015).

6. Under the Irish regime, a transaction is disclosable if it enables a person to obtain a tax advantage which is the main benefit of the transaction and it falls within one of four classes of a specified description: *(1)* Confidentiality; *(2)* Premium fee; *(3)* Standardised documentation; or *(4)* a class or classes of tax advantage (loss schemes, employment schemes, income into capital schemes, income into gift schemes).

7. Those four countries are Canada, Ireland, South Africa and the United Kingdom that have mandatory disclosure regimes. The US statistics are removed from the analysis because the United States only submits publicly available information to the ATP Directory.

Bibliography

OECD (2011), *Tackling Aggressive Tax Planning through Improved Transparency and Disclosure*, OECD, Paris, www.oecd.org/ctp/exchange-of-tax-information/48322860.pdf.

OECD (2008), *Study into the Role of Tax Intermediaries*, OECD Publishing, Paris, http://dx.doi.org/10.1787/9789264041813-en.

Chapter 2

Options for a model mandatory disclosure rule

56. In order to successfully obtain early information about tax planning schemes and the users and promoters of those schemes, certain design features need to be considered when constructing a mandatory disclosure regime. These include: who reports, what information they report and when. Action 12 recognises that the design of a mandatory disclosure regime has to be flexible to the needs and risks in specific countries so this chapter sets out options for a model mandatory disclosure regime. This should allow countries that wish to introduce a mandatory disclosure regime to adopt a modular approach, which is dynamic enough to allow tax administrators to adjust the regime to respond to new risks (or carve-out obsolete risks), and to choose the options that best fit their requirements.

57. Existing mandatory disclosure regimes could be described as falling into two basic categories:

- The first approach, reflected in the approach adopted by the United States, is a *transaction-based* approach. In general terms, this approach to mandatory disclosure begins by identifying transactions that the tax administration considers give rise to tax revenue or policy risks (a reportable scheme) and then requires disclosure from taxpayers who derive a tax benefit from, and any person who provides material assistance in relation to, that reportable scheme.
- The second approach, reflected in the approach adopted by the United Kingdom and Ireland, could be described as a *promoter-based* approach. In general terms, this approach has a greater focus on the role played by promoters of tax planning schemes but it does also consider what types of reportable scheme promoters and taxpayers are required to disclose.

58. To the extent that there is any real difference between these approaches it is reflected in the way in which each regime identifies schemes, taxpayers and promoters and the nature of the disclosure obligations imposed upon them. For example, a promoter-based approach places the primary disclosure obligation on the promoter, whereas a transaction-based approach may place identical disclosure obligations on both taxpayers and promoters. There can also be a difference in the way in which each defines a reportable scheme. For instance, a transaction-based approach will place more reliance on specific hallmarks; while a promoter-based approach, which is more focused on the supply of tax planning schemes, may rely more heavily on generic hallmarks and limit the disclosure to those arrangements where tax is one of the main benefits of the scheme.[1]

59. Although the approaches may have slightly different starting points they cover the same ground and have the same basic set of objectives, design features and effects. Therefore the distinction between transaction and promoter-based approaches may not in reality be that significant. In particular:

- None of the existing mandatory disclosure regimes exhibit a purely transaction or promoter-based approach. For example, as discussed below, whilst the United States imposes the obligation to report on both promoters and taxpayers the mandatory disclosure regime also utilises certain generic hallmarks to tackle promoter behaviour.
- Even when the approaches appear different in practice, they can end up in a similar place. For example, as discussed below, when it comes to the question of "who has to report", the UK promoter-based regime achieves an outcome that is substantially similar to the transaction-based approach by requiring additional disclosure from the taxpayer in the form of scheme identification numbers.

60. Accordingly, while acknowledging the differences between mandatory disclosure regimes, the design recommendations in this chapter are based on the core features common to all these regimes.

Who has to report

Overview

61. Mandatory disclosure regimes need to identify the person who is obliged to disclose under the regime. As highlighted above there are two different approaches based on existing mandatory disclosure regimes: *(1)* to impose the primary obligation to disclose on the promoter; or *(2)* to impose an obligation on both the promoter and the taxpayer. The common feature is that both introduce some obligations on the promoter or material advisor. This reflects the fact that the promoter who designs and sells a scheme inevitably has more information on the scheme and how it works. Imposing an obligation on the promoter also has the advantage of potentially influencing the behaviour of the promoter and having an impact on the supply side of the avoidance market.

Options

62. There are therefore two options:

Box 2.1. **Options for "who has to report"**

- Option A: Both the promoter **and** the taxpayer have the obligation to disclose separately
- Option B: Either the promoter **or** the taxpayer has the obligation to disclose

Option A: Both the promoter and the taxpayer have the obligation to disclose separately

63. The first option places the disclosure obligation on both the promoter and user. Among countries that have mandatory disclosure rules, Canada and the United States adopt this model. However, in Canada, with the proper election, the disclosure by one of the parties can satisfy the obligation of each party whereas, in the United States, taxpayers must provide information about specified transactions in their returns regardless of whether the promoter has previously disclosed the transaction. Equally, in the United States, the obligation of a promoter, who is a material advisor, to provide information about reportable transactions will not be satisfied by a taxpayer's disclosure of the same.

64. The Canadian regime imposes a disclosure obligation for each separate "reportable transaction" of a tax avoidance scheme and imposes the obligation to disclose scheme details equally on taxpayers who derive tax benefits from the transaction as well as promoters and advisors who are entitled to certain fees in respect of the reportable transaction. The filing of a full and accurate disclosure form by any one of the taxpayer, promoter or advisor in respect of a reportable transaction, however, means that the other persons will be treated as having met their separate disclosure obligations in respect of that transaction. In addition, if the transaction is part of a series, the filing of an information return by a person who reports each transaction in the series can be considered to satisfy the obligation of each other person who must file for the series.

65. Under the US disclosure rules, each US taxpayer that has participated in a reportable transaction is required to provide detailed information about the transaction and its expected tax benefits on a separate disclosure statement attached to the taxpayer's tax return and filed concurrently with the Internal Revenue Service (IRS) Office of Tax Shelter Analysis (OTSA).

Option B: Either the promoter or the taxpayer has the obligation to disclose

66. Under this approach promoters have the primary obligation to disclose and if such disclosure is made then users are not, as a general rule, required to provide details of the scheme to the tax administration. In both the United Kingdom and South Africa, the promoter must provide the participant or user with a scheme reference number to put on their return and, in South Africa, the participant's obligation to disclose only falls away when the participant has obtained written confirmation that disclosure has been made by a promoter or another participant.

67. A focus on the promoter as having the primary obligation to disclose may have the advantage of efficiency and, particularly in the context of mass-marketed scheme, it is likely to be the promoter who has a better understanding of the scheme and the tax benefit arising under the scheme. Users are generally required to provide full details of the scheme, however, in circumstances where there is no promoter of the scheme or where the promoter does not disclose or is prevented from disclosing the scheme. The United Kingdom, Portugal, Ireland and South Africa place the primary disclosure obligation on the user in the following circumstances.

(i) Where the promoter is offshore

68. In theory, mandatory disclosure regimes apply equally to all promoters. However, where a scheme involves a promoter based offshore, there are practical difficulties in ensuring compliance so a scheme user is instead required to disclose the scheme details to the tax authority.

(ii) Where there is no promoter

69. Where there is no person who is a promoter in relation to a scheme, it has to be disclosed by the person using the scheme. This could arise, for example, where a scheme is developed by a corporate "in-house". It should be noted, however, that in such cases disclosure only applies to schemes that have actually been implemented.

(iii) Where the promoter asserts legal professional privilege

70. While schemes promoted by legal professionals come within the scope of mandatory disclosure rules, the existing legislation recognises that legal professional privilege, as recognised under the UK and Irish law, may act to prevent the promoter from providing the information required to make a full disclosure.[2] In this circumstance, the obligation to disclose falls on the scheme user. Alternatively, the client has the option of waiving any right to legal privilege and, if that happens, the obligation to disclose remains with the promoter. The legal professional asserting legal privilege must advise clients of their obligation to disclose and must also advise the tax administration that the legal professional's obligation to disclose has not been complied with because of the assertion of legal professional privilege.

Further considerations

71. Under both options the "promoter" or "advisor" will need to be defined. Existing regimes use differing definitions, although there is a degree of overlap, and these definitions are set out in Box 2.2 and summarised in Annex E.

Box 2.2. **Draft definition of promoter or advisor in applicable legislation**

- A "**promoter**" is defined as a person, in the course of a relevant business, who is responsible for the design, marketing, organisation or management of a scheme or who makes a scheme available for implementation by another person.(**UK and Irish legislation**).
- A "**material advisor**" is defined as any person who provides any material aid, assistance or advice with respect to organising, managing, promoting, selling, implementing, insuring, or carrying out any reportable transaction and who directly or indirectly derives gross income in excess of the threshold amounts of USD 50 000 or 250 000 (or 10 000 or 25 000) depending on the type of taxpayer and type of reportable transaction. (**US legislation**).
- An "**advisor**" means a person who provides any contractual protection in respect of a transaction or series of transactions, or any assistance or advice with respect to creating, developing, planning, organising or implementing the transaction or series, to another person. A "**promoter**" means a person who *(a)* promotes or sells an arrangement that includes or relates to a transaction or series of transactions; *(b)* makes a statement or representation that a tax benefit could result from an arrangement in furtherance of the promoting or selling of the arrangement, or *(c)* accepts consideration in respect of an arrangement in paragraph (a) or (b). (**Canadian legislation**).
- A "**promoter**" is defined as a person who is principally responsible for organising, designing, selling, financing or managing the reportable arrangement. (**South African** legislation)
- The common themes or principles within these separate definitions would appear to be as follows:
  - The promoter is any person responsible for or involved in designing, marketing, organising or managing the tax advantage element of any reportable scheme in the course of providing services relating to taxation.
  - This definition can include any person who provides any material aid, assistance or advice with respect to designing, marketing, organising or managing the tax aspects of a transaction that causes the transaction to be a reportable transaction.

72. In addition as both options place an obligation on the promoter there will potentially be a deterrent effect on the supply side of the avoidance market. The benefit of Option A is that it may have a stronger deterrent effect on both the supply (promoter) and demand (user) side of avoidance schemes.

73. This approach also imposes a more extensive disclosure obligation on users compared with Option B and can trigger multiple disclosures of the same transaction. A dual disclosure obligation reduces the risk of inadequate disclosure because, for example, a taxpayer's disclosure can be checked against the promoter's disclosure to assess whether the information provided is accurate and comprehensive.

74. However, the disadvantage of the first option is that it is likely to give rise to greater costs as where a dual disclosure obligation is imposed, tax authorities may require the

taxpayer to file a separate form for each reportable transaction in which the taxpayer participated. Consequently, this approach will increase the administrative and compliance costs for the taxpayer, and potentially those of the tax administration. Whether these increased costs merit the benefits of dual disclosure obligations must be considered in deciding who has to report.

75. The option chosen is likely to have an impact on a country's choices in respect of other elements of a mandatory disclosure regime, for instance if there is a dual reporting obligation which requires both taxpayers and promoters to disclose, there is no need for the use of scheme reference numbers.

Recommendation

76. Countries adopting mandatory disclosure rules will need to decide whether or not they introduce a dual reporting requirement that applies to the promoter and taxpayer or whether they introduce a reporting obligation that falls primarily on the promoter. However, where the primary reporting obligation falls on the promoter it is recommended that the reporting obligation switches to the taxpayer where:

- The promoter is offshore.
- There is no promoter.
- The promoter asserts legal professional privilege.

77. Countries are free to introduce their own definition of promoter or advisor but it is recommended that any definition encompasses the principles set out in Box 2.2. In addition input from relevant domestic stakeholders will be important in order to establish the appropriate promoter definition in a specific jurisdiction, for example to ensure that those who have knowledge of the tax scheme are included but those who provide services incidental to the scheme are not treated as a promoter where they did not have any knowledge as regards the tax elements of the transaction or scheme.

What has to be reported

78. There are two key issues in respect of "what has to be reported". The first issue goes to the substance of a mandatory disclosure regime and focuses on what schemes or arrangements a tax administration wants to know about. The second issue arises if a transaction is reportable and is about the specific information to be disclosed (i.e. name, taxpayer number, details of transaction, etc.). This section describes what types of schemes and arrangements should be disclosed under the regime (i.e. the definition of what is a "reportable scheme"). The second issue is discussed in more detail in the section on procedural/tax administration matters.

Threshold requirement

79. Under existing mandatory disclosure regimes a transaction is reportable if it falls within the descriptions or hallmarks set out in the regime. However, some regimes first apply a threshold or pre-condition that a scheme must satisfy before it is assessed against the hallmarks. Threshold tests may consider whether a transaction has the features of an avoidance scheme or whether a main benefit of the scheme was obtaining a tax advantage.[3]

80. A number of countries such as the United Kingdom, Ireland and Canada impose a threshold requirement or precondition for the application of the regime. A threshold can be used to filter out irrelevant disclosures and may, subject to the concerns highlighted in paragraph 82 below, reduce some of the compliance and administration burden of the regime by targeting only tax motivated transactions that are likely to pose the greatest tax policy and revenue risks. There are different views on the merits of the single-step versus the multi-step or threshold approach. Those who favour the former approach note that a similar effect to the multi-step approach can be achieved under a single step approach through using filters and narrower or more targeted hallmarks so that the two approaches may not be inherently different.

81. One of the key challenges in applying a threshold condition is determining the right threshold. The most common threshold requirement is a main benefit test. Under such a threshold the arrangement must satisfy the condition that the tax advantage is, or might be expected to be the main benefit or one of the main benefits of entering into the arrangement. Such a test compares the value of the expected tax advantage with any other benefits likely to be obtained from the transaction and has the advantage of requiring an objective assessment of the tax benefits. A number of countries consider this to be effective at filtering out all but the most relevant schemes.

82. However, the main benefit test sets a relatively high threshold for disclosure and the experience of at least one country suggests that it can be used inappropriately as a justification for not disclosing tax avoidance schemes that would be of interest to a tax administration. Such a pre-condition may also make enforcement of the disclosure obligations more complex and create uncertain outcomes for taxpayers.

Options

83. Based on the above analysis there appear to be two options:

> Box 2.3. **Multi-step or single step approach to defining the scope of a disclosure regime**
>
> - Option A: Countries adopt a single-step approach
> - Option B: Countries adopt a multi-step or threshold approach

Option A: Adopt a single-step approach

84. As highlighted above countries involved in this work had a range of views on the inclusion of a threshold condition. One option therefore would be to exclude a threshold condition entirely and simply recommend the adoption of a single-step approach. Among countries having mandatory disclosure rules, the United States adopts a single-step approach where the domestic tax benefit does not need to be identified as tax avoidance or as the main benefit of the transaction.

85. There is a concern, however, that a single-step approach could generate a large number of disclosures increasing the costs to both taxpayers and tax administrations and also diluting the relevance of the information received. The amount of disclosures can be controlled, however, by other means such as having narrower or more tightly defined hallmarks and/or by filtering disclosures by reference to a monetary threshold. This

would appear to be the approach adopted in the United States as the number of disclosed transactions is calibrated using specific hallmarks, i.e. listed transactions that are further limited through the use of filters. For instance the US regime uses monetary filters in respect of loss transactions and also includes a monetary filter in the definition of a material advisor. There may therefore be little practical difference in the two approaches in terms of the amount of disclosures received and the choice of approach may be influenced by how well a threshold condition such as a main benefit test will be understood or applied by taxpayers.

Option B: Adopt a multi-step or threshold approach

86. The UK, Irish, Canadian, and Portuguese regimes adopt a multi-step approach and require all schemes to meet a threshold condition as part of their mandatory disclosure regime. The advantage of a multi-step approach is that it separately identifies the tax planning element in each scheme by reference to a common standard and means that hallmarks can be targeted at particular categories of transaction (such as leasing transactions) without the need to separately identify and define any tax planning element. This flexibility is particularly relevant in the context of generic hallmarks that do not necessarily identify a separate tax motivated part. It was, however, recognised that a precondition that focuses on a tax benefit may not work well in the context of international schemes so those countries who apply a pre-condition may need to limit its application to domestic schemes and adopt a single-step framework for the mandatory disclosure of international schemes. There is further discussion of this in Chapter 3. Concerns that the threshold condition may be used by taxpayers to justify non-disclosure could be addressed by lowering the threshold for disclosure or exempting certain hallmarks from the threshold requirement. This latter approach is one that has been adopted in South Africa which excludes arrangements where the tax benefit is not the main or one of the main benefits unless the arrangement is listed (i.e. equivalent to specific hallmarks), in which case it is reportable, regardless of whether it satisfies the main benefit test.

De-minimis filter

87. A de-minimis filter could be considered as an alternative to, or in addition to, a broader threshold test and could operate to remove smaller transactions, below a certain amount, from the disclosure requirements. It would therefore narrow the ambit of the mandatory disclosure regime and reduce the risk of over-disclosure. It may also enhance the usefulness of the information collected because the focus would be on more significant transactions and excessive or defensive filings could be reduced. This could reduce the costs and administrative burden for certain taxpayers and for the tax administration.

88. In addition a de-minimis filter could be applied to all transactions potentially within scope or just to certain categories of transactions where there might otherwise be large numbers of reportable transactions. Different threshold amounts could also be applied to specific hallmarks to calibrate the disclosures in a particular area and some countries already adopt this approach. For instance, in the US regime, reportable loss transactions have their own dollar thresholds. The thresholds range from USD 50 000 to USD 10 million, depending on the taxpayer and the type of loss transaction.

89. However, consideration would need to be given to what element a de-minimis filter would apply to, that is, should it be applied to the amount of the tax advantage or the value of the transaction? There could also be concerns that, if not carefully drafted, the filter could be used to circumvent the disclosure obligation and may create additional

complexity in the application of the rules. Additionally including a de-minimis filter could unhelpfully suggest that tax avoidance, in small amounts, is acceptable and there may in fact be little or no correlation between the size of a transaction and its relative interest to a tax administration. For instance a new or innovative transaction could be initially "tested" on a small scale and if that transaction is not reported until it occurs on a wider scale then a de-minimis limit will simply delay the time when a tax administration receives information and can act against a scheme. Additionally the nature of the transaction may remove any concerns that the transaction is low level or insignificant, this could be the case if mandatory disclosure regimes picked up international transactions.

90. Based on the above analysis it was concluded that a de-minimis test would sit poorly alongside any pre-condition based on a main benefit test as, in this situation, a regime is already targeting transactions that were designed to generate a tax benefit so a further filter is unnecessary. However a de-minimis filter could be easier to apply, and have a clearer impact, where it is used in conjunction with a specific hallmark as is the case in the United States. The level of any threshold would then be left to the discretion of individual tax administrations and could help reduce the level of disclosures under a specific hallmark, if these are expected to be numerous.

Hallmarks

91. Hallmarks act as tools to identify the features of schemes that tax administrations are interested in. They are generally divided into two categories: generic and specific hallmarks. Generic hallmarks target features that are common to promoted schemes, such as the requirement for confidentiality or the payment of a premium fee. Generic hallmarks can also be used to capture new and innovative tax planning arrangements that may be easily replicated and sold to a variety of taxpayers. Specific hallmarks are used to target known vulnerabilities in the tax system and techniques that are commonly used in tax avoidance arrangements such as the use of losses.

Outline of generic hallmarks

92. Two typical generic hallmarks used for targeting promoted schemes are:

- "Confidentiality" hallmarks where the promoter or adviser requires the client to keep the scheme confidential.
- "Premium fee" or "contingent fee" hallmarks where the amount the client pays for the advice can be attributed to the value of the tax benefits obtained under the scheme.

93. Other hallmarks which are less frequently used include "contractual protection" where the parties agree an allocation of risk in respect of a failure of the tax consequences of the scheme and "standardised tax product" intended to capture widely-marketed schemes.

Confidentiality

94. A confidential scheme is one that is offered to the adviser's clients under conditions of confidentiality. The confidentiality obligation is owed by the client to the promoter (not by the promoter to the client). The promoter might, for example, place a limitation

on the disclosure by the taxpayer of the tax treatment or tax structure. This limitation on disclosure is to protect the value of the scheme designed by the promoter.

95. A confidentiality condition indicates that a promoter or a corporate wishes to keep schemes or arrangements confidential either from other promoters or from the tax authorities. This implies that the arrangements may be innovative or aggressive. A confidentiality condition enables a promoter or a corporate to sell the same scheme to a number of different taxpayers.

96. The use of a confidentiality clause in an agreement may mean that the hallmark is met. However, even if certain promoters use such a clause or condition, tax authorities might accept that the confidentiality hallmark was not met if the scheme is reasonably well-known in the tax community. This is the United Kingdom's approach.

Premium or Contingent fee

97. The "premium fee" clause is also one of the most common generic hallmarks. Versions of these hallmarks are found in the UK, US, Irish and Canadian regimes. It is designed to capture those schemes that have been sold on the basis of the tax benefits that accrue under them. The UK, Irish and Canadian regimes target both "premium fees" and fees that are contingent on the tax benefits that arise under the scheme (i.e. contingent fees).

98. Under the UK rule, the hallmark referred to as "premium fee" tries to capture arrangements from which a promoter could obtain an increased (premium) fee. A premium fee is a fee that is to a significant extent attributable to the tax advantage, or to any extent contingent upon obtaining that tax advantage. The idea of a premium fee is that there is an amount payable that is attributable both to the value of the tax advice and the fact that it is not available anywhere else. However if the consequences of the scheme are widely-known and understood then the client would be unwilling to pay more than a normal fee for it.

99. While the fee hallmark in the US legislation is referred to as "contractual protection" it is similar to the contingency fee hallmark in that it covers the situation where a taxpayer or a related party has the right to a full or partial refund of fees if the intended tax consequences are not obtained, and it applies if the fees are contingent on the taxpayers receiving tax benefits from the scheme.

100. Some countries have suggested that, in certain circumstances a premium fee can be replaced by an increased charge that is built into the transaction itself (rather than a separate fee for legal or tax advice) and that this concept should be captured by the definition of premium fee. However, other countries consider that the definition of a premium fee should be broad enough to capture these types of charges while a few have suggested that such a broad definition may raise compliance difficulties and that such schemes may be better targeted with other types of hallmarks. Countries will wish to consider these definitional and compliance issues when setting the definition of premium fee.

Contractual protection

101. A contractual protection clause is used as a generic hallmark in Canada and Portugal. In Canada, contractual protection means *(1)* any form of insurance (other than standard professional liability insurance) or other protection such as an indemnity or compensation that *(i)* protects against a failure of the transaction to result in any portion of the tax benefit being sought from the transaction, or *(ii)* pays for or reimburses any expense, fee,

tax, interest, penalty or similar amount that may be incurred in the course of a dispute in respect of a tax benefit arising from the transaction; and *(2)* any form of undertaking provided by a promoter that provides assistance to the taxpayer in the course of a dispute in respect of a tax benefit from the transaction.

102. In Portugal, there is one generic hallmark which is used in order to determine whether any transaction falls within the mandatory disclosure rule. This hallmark captures transactions with a clause waiving or limiting the liability of a promoter.

Standardised tax products

103. This hallmark is intended to capture what are often referred to as 'mass-marketed schemes' and is used as a generic hallmark in the UK and Irish regimes. A 'mass-marketed scheme' means an arrangement that is made available to more than one person and that uses standardised documentation that is not tailored to any material extent to the client's circumstances.

104. The fundamental characteristic of such schemes is their ease of replication. Schemes with this replication characteristic have variously been described as 'shrink-wrapped' or 'plug and play' schemes. Essentially, all the client purchases is a prepared tax product that requires little, if any, modification to suit their circumstances. The adoption of the scheme does not require the taxpayer to receive significant additional professional advice or services.

105. Korea has a similar hallmark to the standardised tax product hallmark. The Korean mandatory disclosure regime is targeted at standardised 'financial' products which have a tax benefit. A financial tax product is typically one that is mass-marketed and where a number of participants enter into substantially the same contractual arrangements. Such products are mainly tax driven and it is therefore highly unlikely that the financial product would be sold without the tax benefit. The Korean mandatory disclosure regime therefore requires financial institutions which have designed financial products containing tax benefits such as exemption and a reduced rate of withholding tax to disclose the product to the tax authorities before selling it to investors in the financial market.

Model generic hallmarks

106. Most countries agreed that a mandatory disclosure regime should include a combination of generic and specific hallmarks and that a transaction should be reported if it met just one hallmark. Boxes 2.4 and 2.5 include some of the generic hallmarks included in existing mandatory disclosure regimes and combine these into some common principles that could be used to draft "model" generic hallmarks. Countries wishing to introduce mandatory disclosure rules could use these as a base for their generic hallmarks but could revise and adapt them to fit with a country's domestic law.

107. It should be noted that most generic hallmarks (with the exception of the United States) have been designed to operate subject to a threshold requirement that considers whether the transaction has features of a tax avoidance scheme or whether a main benefit of the scheme was obtaining a tax advantage. Therefore further consideration may need to be given to whether such hallmarks would operate equally effectively where there was no such threshold, or whether changes would need to be made to appropriately limit the number of disclosures generated.[4]

Confidentiality

108. A confidentiality hallmark is used in four mandatory disclosure regimes (the United Kingdom, the United States, Canada and Ireland) and given its potential to capture new and innovative tax planning it seems to be a key hallmark. The United Kingdom, and Ireland use a hypothetical version of this hallmark and this is discussed below.

Box 2.4. **Hallmarks for confidentiality**

- **A confidential transaction** is a transaction that is offered to a taxpayer under conditions of confidentiality and the advisor is paid a minimum fee. The amount of the fee is USD 250 000 if the taxpayer is a corporation and USD 50 000 for all other taxpayers. A transaction is considered to be offered under conditions of confidentiality if the advisor who is paid a minimum fee places a limitation on a taxpayer's disclosure of the tax treatment or tax structure of the transaction to any person and the limitation on disclosure protects the confidentiality of the advisor's tax strategies. The transaction is treated as confidential even if the conditions of confidentiality are not legally binding on a taxpayer. A claim that a transaction is proprietary or exclusive is not treated as a limitation on disclosure if the advisor confirms to the taxpayer that there is no limitation on disclosure of the tax treatment or tax structure of the transaction. (**US legislation**).
- **Confidential protection** means anything that prohibits the disclosure, to any person, of the details or structure of the transaction or series under which a tax benefit results. (**Canadian legislation**).
- **Confidential arrangements** are those where it might reasonably be expected that a promoter would wish to keep the way in which any element of those arrangements secures, or might secure, a tax advantage confidential from any other promoter or a tax authority. Such arrangements will fall within the hallmark where a reason for keeping any element of them confidential is to facilitate repeated or continued use of the same element, or substantially the same element, in the future. (**UK and Irish legislation**).
- The common themes or principles within these hallmarks would appear to be as follows:
  - The scheme or arrangement is offered to the taxpayer under conditions of confidentiality.
  - This places a limitation on the taxpayer's disclosure of the tax treatment, the tax structure of the transaction or on the resulting tax benefit.
  - This limitation protects the tax advisor's strategies and may enable further use of the same scheme or transaction.

Premium or contingency fee

109. Premium or contingency fee hallmarks are found in the UK, US, Irish and Canadian regimes. Whilst a premium fee hallmark is slightly different to the contractual protection hallmark used in Canada and Portugal there is some commonality as both are looking at the expected outcomes from a transaction and whether or not these are achieved. It may not therefore be necessary to include both premium fee and contractual protection hallmarks in a mandatory disclosure regime. As noted above, a premium fee may not be a separate charge but could be built into the cost of the transaction itself.

Box 2.5. **Hallmarks for contingency fee/premium fee**

- **A transaction with a contingency fee hallmark** (subject to certain exceptions), is a transaction for which a taxpayer has the right to a full refund or partial refund of fees if all or part of the intended tax consequences from the transaction are not sustained. It also includes a transaction for which fees are contingent on the taxpayer's realisation of tax benefits from the transaction. (**US legislation** – described as **"contractual protection"**)
- **A premium fee** means a fee chargeable by virtue of any element of the arrangements from which the tax advantage expected to be obtained arises; and which is *(a)* to a significant extent attributable to that tax advantage, or *(b)* to any extent contingent upon the obtaining of that tax advantage. **(UK and Irish legislation)**
- **A tax results oriented fee** is a fee which an advisor or promoter is entitled to receive in respect of an avoidance transaction and the fee is *(a)* based on the amount of the tax benefit obtained from the transaction; *(b)* contingent upon the obtaining of a tax benefit from the transaction; or *(c)* attributable to the number of taxpayers who participate in the transaction or have been given access to advice by the advisor or promoter. **(Canadian legislation)**
- The common principles within these hallmarks would appear to be:
  - The taxpayer's fee for the scheme or transaction is directly based on, or linked to the amount of, the tax benefit they expect to receive.
  - If the expected tax outcome is not achieved this may affect the amount of the fee that the taxpayer pays.

Hypothetical application of generic hallmarks

110. Under the UK and Irish regimes, the confidentiality and premium fee hallmark targets not only schemes that are sold to clients for a premium fee but also schemes that could be sold by a promoter for a premium fee. The scope of the hallmark is extended in this way by effectively posing a hypothetical question:

- "Might it reasonably be expected that any promoter of the arrangements would wish the way in which any element of those arrangements gives rise to a tax advantage to be kept confidential from any other promoter." (Confidentiality)
- "Might it reasonably be expected that a promoter would be able to obtain a premium fee from a person experienced in receiving services of the type being provided." (Premium fee)

111. In terms of applying hypothetical tests the confidentiality hallmark would be met if a scheme was sufficiently new and innovative such that an adviser who designed the scheme would have required the details of the scheme to remain confidential irrespective of the existence of actual terms of confidentiality. The use of an explicit confidentiality agreement may indicate that this test is met. However, even where there is a confidentiality clause it may be clear from, for example articles in the tax press, textbooks or case law, that the scheme is in fact well known in the tax community. In the United Kingdom the factors that should be considered include:[5]

- How new, innovative and aggressive the scheme is. Schemes known to the tax administration are not caught by the confidentiality hallmark. The fact that a scheme is known can be evidenced by, for example, technical guidance notes, case law, or past correspondence with the tax administration.

- Whether a promoter imposes an obligation upon potential clients, whether in writing or verbally, to keep the details of the scheme confidential from third parties including the tax administration.
- Whether confidentiality agreements between a promoter and client allow the client to disclose information to the tax administration without referral to the promoter.
- The use of explicit warnings in marketing material or other communications to a client to the effect that the scheme may have a limited "shelf life" because legislative changes may close the scheme once it becomes known.

112. In terms of the hypothetical version of the premium fee test, it is important to look at the value of the scheme from the client's perspective. Where a client regards the advice as valuable and not generally available, then the client might be prepared to pay a premium for it. It is not conclusive that the advisor does not charge a premium fee for the advice. By contrast, if similar tax advice was available elsewhere it is assumed that the client would be unwilling to pay more than a normal fee for it. Therefore, the question is whether it might reasonably be expected that a promoter could charge a premium fee if he wished to do so. At the same time, it is also necessary to consider whether a fee could be charged in respect of any element of the tax arrangement such that it would to a significant extent be attributable to, or contingent upon, the expected tax advantage. For instance in the United Kingdom, a fee is not a premium fee solely on account of factors such as:[6]

- The adviser's location – e.g. fees could be expected to be higher in say London.
- The urgency of the advice – a fee that is higher due to the adviser having to give the advice urgently is not a premium fee for that reason alone.
- The size of the transaction – if a large amount is at stake on a deal, the tax adviser may wish to increase his fee to reflect the greater level of exposure.
- The skill or reputation of the adviser – some advisers normally charge more for advice than others to reflect the perceived higher quality of the advice they offer.
- The scarcity of appropriately skilled staff – some areas of tax advice are more complex and fees may be higher to reflect this.

113. The use of hypothetical tests can broaden the scope of generic hallmarks and may prevent circumvention of hallmarks drafted in a more objective way. Hypothetical tests may also be useful in capturing tax planning schemes that are specifically designed for a particular taxpayer and transaction (bespoke transactions).

114. On the other hand, the generic hallmarks used by the United States, Canada and Portugal do not have hypothetical tests and therefore provide more certainty since the disclosure requirement can be judged based on the existence of an actual confidentiality or premium fee agreement. This objective enquiry into the actual arrangements between adviser and client maybe an easier test for the taxpayer and promoter to apply than the hypothetical question posed in the United Kingdom, and Ireland. It may also be easier for a tax administration to apply an objective test rather than potentially spending time evaluating whether or not transactions should or should not be disclosed.

Options

115. Whilst most countries involved in this work expressed a preference for objective hallmarks several thought that there was a role for subjective tests to prevent circumvention of the disclosure provisions. Both objective and subjective tests are therefore included as an option. However, tax administrations will need to consider the workability of hypothetical or subjective tests in the context of their own domestic tax system.

Box 2.6. **Options for designing generic hallmarks**

- Option A: Adopt hypothetical/subjective hallmarks
- Option B: Adopt objective hallmarks

Option A: adopt hypothetical/subjective hallmarks

116. Those countries who see benefits in a hypothetical test and think that the potential uncertainty and any additional administrative burden are outweighed by better disclosure may want to consider an approach similar to that adopted by the United Kingdom and Ireland. Although consideration would need to be given to how such an approach would operate in the context of their own domestic law and within their tax compliance framework.

Option B: adopt objective hallmarks

117. If countries are less concerned about circumvention, and key design issues for their tax administration are greater certainty and ease of operation, then objective hallmarks may be more suitable.

Specific hallmarks

118. Generic hallmarks such as confidentiality and standardised tax products can target schemes that promoters replicate and sell to more than one person. Therefore, they can obtain information about formulaic and mass-marketed transactions in addition to those that are new and innovative. On the other hand, specific hallmarks reflect the particular or current concerns of tax authorities, and can therefore target areas of perceived high risk such as the use of losses, leasing and income conversion schemes. Specific hallmarks can also be a useful way of keeping a disclosure regime up to date. Some countries such as South Africa have found that specific hallmarks can be more effective in collecting relevant information than generic hallmarks. Reflecting that, different countries may benefit from different combinations of hallmarks.

119. Under specific hallmarks, the disclosure obligation is triggered by describing certain potentially aggressive or abusive transactions and including them as a hallmark. While specific hallmarks are designed to target particular transactions, or particular elements of a transaction, they should be drafted broadly and avoid providing too much in the way of technical detail. Overly narrow or technical hallmarks can be given a restrictive interpretation by taxpayers or may provide opportunities for taxpayers and promoters to structure around their disclosure obligations. Given Action Item 12's reference to a modular design and the fact that risks will differ between countries then this is an area where countries may need maximum flexibility to design their own specific hallmarks. Examples of specific hallmarks used in existing regimes are set out below.

Loss schemes (the United States, the United Kingdom, Canada, Ireland, Portugal)

120. This hallmark is intended to capture various loss creation schemes. The schemes vary considerably in detail but are normally designed so as to provide all or some of the individual participants with losses that will be used to reduce their income tax or capital gains tax liabilities or to generate a repayment. For example, the Canadian tax shelter regime[7] includes the acquisition of property or a gifting arrangement for which representations are made that losses, deduction, or credits in the first four years would be equal to or greater than the net cost of the property invested or acquired under the gifting arrangement. Versions of specific hallmarks involving loss transactions are also found in the United Kingdom, Ireland and the United States.

121. This type of hallmark could be coupled with a threshold applied to the amount of the loss. For example, in the United States, a loss transaction is a transaction that results in a taxpayer claiming a loss that equals or exceeds a threshold amount ranging from USD 50 000 to 10 million in any single taxable year depending on the type of taxpayer and the transaction.

Leasing arrangements (the United Kingdom)

122. This hallmarks aims to capture tax advantages gained from leasing transactions. The hallmark only applies if the arrangement includes a high value plant or machinery lease. Arrangements to lease assets with an individual value of GBP 10 million or an aggregate value of at least 25 million are caught by this test. The hallmark only applies where the lease term is longer than two years. Additionally any one of the three additional conditions needs to be met: *(1)* the lease arrangement involves a party outside the charge to corporation tax; *(2)* the lease arrangement removes the whole or the greater part of the risk from the lessor; *(3)* the lease arrangement involves a finance leaseback.

Employment scheme (Ireland)

123. This specific hallmark targets employment schemes which may seek to use vehicles such as employee benefit trusts or schemes that in some fashion seek to circumvent salary sacrifice anti-avoidance provisions.

Converting income schemes (Ireland, Portugal)

124. This hallmark addresses schemes for converting income into capital or gifts in order to avoid the higher rate of income tax and to have the gain taxed at a lower rate or relieved or exempted from tax in the case of Ireland.

125. In Portugal, this hallmark covers insurance or financial transactions that may give rise to a reclassification of the income or to a change in its recipients and in particular this is aimed at finance leasing, transactions concerning hybrid instruments, derivatives or contracts on financial instruments. There is some overlap with the UK hallmark (leasing arrangements) in terms of involving finance leasing.

Schemes involving entities located in low-tax jurisdictions (Portugal)

126. This hallmark aims to capture schemes involving entities located in low-tax jurisdictions. The term "low-tax jurisdiction" includes an entity located in a listed tax haven, an entity located in a country where there is no corporate income tax or the tax paid

is less than 60% of the applicable standard corporate income tax or involves an entity that benefits from a partial or total tax exemption.

Arrangements involving hybrid instruments (South Africa)

127. This hallmark covers any arrangements that would have qualified as a 'hybrid equity instrument' as defined in the relevant tax legislation. These are essentially transactions involving redeemable preference shares and normal shares where the rights attaching to such shares differ from the rights normally attached to ordinary shares. This hallmark also targets any arrangements that would have qualified as a 'hybrid debt instrument' as defined in the relevant tax legislation, if the prescribed period in that section had been ten years. This is essentially aimed at convertible loan/debenture arrangements (excluding listed debt instruments).

Transactions with significant book-tax differences (the United States)

128. The United States previously included this transaction as a category of reportable transactions. It covered transactions with a USD 10 million book-tax difference (i.e. a difference between tax accounting and financial accounting). The IRS and Treasury Department subsequently determined that including transactions with significant book-tax differences as reportable transactions was not necessary after the issuance of the Schedule M-3, "Net Income (Loss) Reconciliation for Corporations with Total Assets of $10 Million or More"[8] which provides the IRS with detailed information on transactions with significant book-tax differences.

Listed transactions (the United States)

129. The United States requires any "listed transaction" to be disclosed in accordance with its reportable transaction rules. A listed transaction is a transaction that is the same as or substantially similar to one that the IRS has determined to be a tax avoidance transaction and has been identified by IRS notice or other form of published guidance.

Transactions of interest (the United States)

130. The United States requires any "transaction of interest" (TOI) to be disclosed in accordance with its reportable transaction rules. A TOI is a transaction that the IRS and the Treasury Department believe is a transaction that has the potential for tax avoidance or evasion, but for which they lack sufficient information to determine whether the transaction should be identified specifically as a tax avoidance transaction.

Model hallmark for loss transaction

131. A common area of concern is losses; schemes involving losses vary considerably in detail but are normally designed so that they generate trading losses for wealthy individuals or corporates that can then be offset against their income tax (including capital gains tax) liabilities. Given the variety of loss schemes, and the recognition that countries will need maximum flexibility in drafting specific hallmarks, setting out common principles may be less helpful in this context. However some principles, along with summaries of the existing legislative provisions, are set out in Box 2.7.

Box 2.7. **Hallmarks for loss transaction**

- A loss transaction is a transaction that results in taxpayer claiming a loss if the amount of the loss exceeds a certain amount depending on the type of taxpayer. (**US legislation**)
- A loss transaction is prescribed if *(a)* the promoter expects more than one individual to implement the same, or substantially the same, transaction; and *(b)* the transaction is such that it could be reasonably concluded that the main benefit of the transaction is the provision of losses and that those individuals would be expected to use those losses to reduce their income tax liability. (**UK legislation** – this hallmark is intended to capture loss schemes that are typically used by wealthy individuals)
- A loss transaction is prescribed if one of the parties to the scheme is a company that has or expects to have unrelieved losses at the end of an accounting period and it could be reasonably concluded that *(a)* the main benefit of the scheme is that the company transfers those losses to another party which would be expected to use them to reduce its corporation tax liability, or *(b)* the company is able to accelerate the use of those losses to reduce its corporation tax liability. (**Irish legislation** – the hallmark is expanded to deal with company losses)
- With the exception of the United States which focusses exclusively on the amount of the loss, the common principles would appear to be that a person incurs or acquires a loss and that loss:
  - is transferred to another person to set off against other income and reduce their tax liability;
  - is accelerated to reduce the current tax liability of a person;
  - is part of a promoted scheme or transaction, used by more than one person, to reduce tax on their other income.

Recommendations on hallmarks

132. Generic hallmarks may increase the amount of reportable transactions, potentially increasing costs for taxpayers but, as already mentioned, they are a useful tool for capturing new and innovative transactions which specific hallmarks have difficulty in capturing. The use of generic hallmarks such as premium fee, confidentiality and contractual protection therefore appear to be key in enabling tax administrations to detect and react quickly to new schemes. Requiring the reporting of these types of transactions may also have the effect of reducing such transactions in the market.

133. Specific hallmarks or listed transactions allow tax administrations to target known or common areas of risk. They also appear to provide flexibility in terms of enabling a tax administration to strike a balance between costs and capacity issues for the tax administration and the reporting burden on promoters or taxpayers. Some countries such as South Africa have found that specific hallmarks can be more effective in collecting relevant information than generic hallmarks. Reflecting that, different countries may benefit from different combinations of hallmarks.

134. Specific hallmarks can also be a useful way of keeping a disclosure regime up to date and for dealing with avoidance on non-mainstream taxes. As can be seen from the existing specific hallmarks, whilst there is some level of overlap, such hallmarks generally reflect the key risk areas in a given jurisdiction.

Recommendations

135. Where countries introduce a mandatory disclosure regime they have the option to use a single-step approach or a multi-step/threshold approach. It is, however, recommended that mandatory disclosure regimes include a mixture of generic and specific hallmarks. Generic hallmarks should include a confidentiality and premium/contingent fee hallmark. A country may also want to adopt additional generic hallmarks such as the one applying to standardised tax products.

136. Countries can choose whether or not to adopt a hypothetical approach or adopt purely factual objectives tests. Specific hallmarks should reflect the particular risks and issues in individual countries. The design and selection of specific hallmarks should be left to each country taking into account their own tax policy and enforcement priorities. Countries are free to choose whether or not specific hallmarks are linked to a de-minimis amount to limit the number of disclosures.

137. It is recommended that where a scheme or transaction triggers one hallmark that should be sufficient to require disclosure.

When information is reported

138. There are significant differences as to when countries require disclosure of schemes. Timing depends on the relevant trigger event and the time period for reporting allowed under the regime. This time period can vary from within days, months, or longer.

139. If the main objectives of a disclosure regime are to provide early information on avoidance schemes and their users and to deter the use of those schemes then the timeframe within which a disclosure has to be made will be important in achieving these objectives as the earlier the reporting, the more quickly a tax administration can act against a scheme. This may enhance the deterrent effects by reducing the time available to take advantage of any tax benefit, so altering the economics of the transaction.

140. There are several questions that need to be considered in setting the timeframe for disclosure and the answers to these questions will impact on the timeliness of a disclosure and may impact on the ability of a disclosure regime to meet some of its objectives. The questions are:

- At what point should the obligation to disclose start, or, to put it another way, what event or action triggers the need to report?
- How soon after that event should a disclosure be made?
- Should there be different reporting timeframes for promoters and taxpayers?

Options for timing of promoter disclosure

Box 2.8. **Options for timing of promoter disclosure**

- Option A: Timeframe linked to availability of a scheme
- Option B: Timeframe linked to implementation

Timeframe linked to availability of a scheme

141. The earliest event that can realistically trigger a disclosure requirement is the point at which a promoter makes a scheme available to users. At this point the scheme will be sufficiently well-developed to be marketable and all the necessary information on how the scheme works must be available if it is being promoted and sold. Under the UK legislation a scheme is regarded as "made available for implementation" at the point when all the elements necessary for implementation of the scheme are in place and a communication is made to a client suggesting that the client might consider entering into transactions forming part of the scheme, it does not matter whether full details of the scheme are communicated at that time. Further details on how this operates in the United Kingdom are included in Annex A.

142. The UK, Irish and Portuguese disclosure regimes all use this as the trigger event. However, the timescale within which the disclosure must then be made differs between the three countries. In the United Kingdom and Ireland a promoter must disclose a scheme within five working days of making a scheme available for implementation by another person. Therefore both the trigger event and the reporting period are designed to ensure a quick disclosure which may well take place before the users have implemented the scheme. This maximises a tax administration's ability to risk assess schemes early and if necessary to take legislative action to close any loopholes before significant amounts of revenue can be lost.

143. Whilst Portugal uses the same trigger event the timescale for reporting is slightly longer as tax promoters who are involved in any tax planning must disclose within 20 days following the end of the month in which the scheme was made available. Again this also ensures a relatively quick disclosure but it is less likely that the tax administration is aware of the scheme before it is implemented which could ultimately impact on the amount of any revenue loss.

144. In the United States instead of linking the disclosure period directly to the point at which the scheme is made available to users the disclosure requirement is triggered on an advisor becoming a "material advisor". A material advisor is defined as a person who provides any material aid, assistance or advice with respect to organising, promoting, or carrying out any reportable transaction and who directly or indirectly receives or is expected to receive gross income in excess of the threshold amount of USD 50 000 or 250 000 (lowered to USD 10 000 and 25 000 for listed transactions) depending on the type of taxpayer and the type of reportable transaction. A person becomes a material advisor when all of the following events occur in no particular order: *(1)* the person provided material aid, advice or assistance with respect to a reportable transaction; *(2)* the person indirectly or directly derived fees in excess of the threshold; *(3)* the taxpayer entered into the reportable transaction; and *(4)* in the case of a listed transaction or transaction of interest the guidance is published identifying the transaction as such. Again there is a link to the actions of the material advisor and reference to activities that either make a scheme available or enable its implementation. However the timescale for reporting in the United States is different in that a material advisor is required to file a disclosure statement with the IRS OTSA by the last day of the month that follows the end of the calendar quarter in which the advisor became a material advisor with respect to the reportable transaction. This can introduce a longer timescale particularly when compared to that in the United Kingdom and Ireland.

Timeframe linked to implementation

145. A disclosure regime could also link the reporting requirement to when a scheme has been implemented by users. At this point it is more likely that there is a real tax loss but there is also limited potential to influence the taxpayer's behaviour which means that the overall revenue loss could be greater.

146. Under the South African regime a reportable arrangement must be disclosed within 45 days after the date that any amount is first received by or accrued to a taxpayer or is paid or actually incurred by a taxpayer in terms of that arrangement. The disclosure obligation is therefore triggered where there is receipt or payment of money, for a transaction forming part of a reportable arrangement; this effectively shows that the arrangement has been implemented.

147. In Canada a reportable transaction must be disclosed by 30 June of the calendar year following that in which the transaction became a reportable transaction. A reportable transaction is an avoidance transaction that meets at least two of the hallmarks in the Canadian regime. The timeframe for reporting is therefore triggered by the transaction becoming reportable. This would occur once it has been implemented. This trigger event combined with a long reporting timescale means that information is received much later than under the UK, Irish and Portuguese regimes. This will inevitably impact on a tax administration's ability to react quickly, potentially leading to greater revenue loss and a reduced deterrent effect.

Options for timing of taxpayer disclosure

148. As discussed in this chapter existing mandatory disclosure regimes either require both the promoter and the taxpayer to disclose (the United States and Canada) or they put the primary obligation on the promoter and only require the taxpayer to disclose where there is no promoter or the promoter is unlikely to disclose, for instance, because the promoter is offshore (the United Kingdom, Ireland, Portugal and South Africa).

149. Similar policy considerations would seem to apply to the timing of a disclosure by a taxpayer as apply to the promoter, that is: the earlier the disclosure, the greater the ability of a disclosure regime to meet its objectives. However this is especially true where there is no promoter disclosure and only the taxpayer discloses.

150. In the United States the taxpayer reports their involvement in a reportable scheme as part of the tax return process and with the IRS OTSA (which is where any material advisor should also have sent its disclosure) the first time that the taxpayer reports the transaction on their tax return. In the US experience, taxpayer reporting that is not tied to the time a tax return is due is often inadvertently overlooked or missed.[9] In Canada the reporting requirement is the same for taxpayers and promoters. In both situations the requirement to report effectively arises after a scheme has been implemented and the timescale for reporting is such that there could be significant time lag between implementation and subsequent disclosure.

151. The United Kingdom, Ireland, Portugal and South Africa only require the taxpayer to disclose in relatively limited circumstances. But when the taxpayer is required to report the scheme then, unlike the situation in the United States and Canada, that will be the only disclosure made. The United Kingdom, Ireland and Portugal all modify both the trigger event and the period within which a disclosure must be made in the case of a taxpayer disclosure. For instance for "in house" schemes both the UK and Irish regimes require a taxpayer to disclose within 30 days from the date of the first transaction entered into by

the user. So the reporting period is triggered by implementation and the taxpayer is given slightly longer to report. Similar modifications apply in Portugal where users are required to report a scheme before the end of the month following the month of implementation. The definition of "implementation" needs to identify the point at which it is clear that a transaction will proceed, this will provide certainty but also prevent taxpayers from artificially delaying disclosure.

152. Where only the taxpayer/user reports then it seems sensible to link the reporting requirement to implementation because it is difficult to identify another point or event that provides an objective trigger for the reporting obligation. It would be possible to use a more subjective trigger, such as the point at which the taxpayer decided to undertake the transaction. This could lead to an earlier disclosure than a reporting period linked to implementation but it would also provide less certainty for the taxpayer and may be difficult to administer.

153. The South African regime applies the same timeframe for a taxpayer as promoter and therefore a taxpayer must disclose a reportable arrangement within 45 days after an amount has first been received by or accrued to a taxpayer or is first paid or actually incurred by a taxpayer.

154. Whilst the timeframe for a taxpayer disclosure in the United Kingdom, Ireland and Portugal is longer than that allowed for a promoter, it is still designed to generate an early disclosure thus enabling the tax administration to react more quickly.

Further considerations

155. It could be argued that there is less need to have early disclosure if a government is unable to react quickly to change their legislation and the administrative constraints on each tax administration do need to be taken into account. However, whilst this is a relevant consideration there are many ways in which governments and tax administrations can influence taxpayer behaviour, they could for instance publish a view on a scheme or transaction if they think it does not work. Additionally the bigger the gap between a scheme being marketed and the eventual disclosure the more users there will be. The tax administration will therefore need to challenge more cases, potentially tying up resources and if the scheme is successful there will be a greater loss of tax revenues. Therefore the countries involved in this work agreed that the timeframe for disclosure should be as efficient as possible within the context of their domestic law.

Recommendations

156. It is recommended that where the promoter has the obligation to disclose then the timeframe for disclosure should be linked to the availability of the scheme and that the timescale for disclosure should aim to maximise the tax administration's ability to react to the scheme quickly and to influence taxpayers' behaviour. This would be achieved by setting a short timescale for reporting once a scheme is available.

157. Where a taxpayer has to disclose it is recommended that the disclosure is triggered by implementation rather than availability of a scheme. In addition if only the taxpayer discloses (i.e. because there is no promoter or the promoter is offshore) the timescale for reporting should be short to maximise the tax administration's ability to act against a scheme quickly.

Other obligations to be placed on the promoters or users

Process of identifying scheme users

158. Identifying scheme users is an essential part of any mandatory disclosure regime and existing regimes identify these in two ways: *(1)* through the use of scheme reference numbers which enable them to identify which taxpayer has used a specific scheme; or, *(2)* instead of (or in addition to) using an identifying number, they impose an obligation on the promoter to provide a list of clients who have made use of a disclosed scheme.[10]

159. Where a scheme reference number is used, the process will generally need to cover three steps:

- The tax authority issues a scheme reference number to a promoter or the users (as appropriate).
- The promoter provides the scheme reference number to the users.
- The users report the scheme reference numbers to the tax authority when the users submit their tax returns.

These three steps are discussed in a little more detail below.

160. The reference number is issued by the tax authority at the time the scheme is disclosed and is provided to the person who disclosed the scheme. Where the scheme reference number is given to a promoter, he must then provide the reference number to a scheme user within a given timeframe (the United Kingdom provides a 30-day deadline and the United States gives 60 calendar days). Where the user is the person required to disclose the scheme then the tax authority will allocate a scheme reference number directly to the user.

161. The user must then include the scheme reference number on their tax return. For instance in the United Kingdom, the number must be entered on the return that relates to the year of assessment, tax year, accounting period or earnings period (as the case may be) in which the user first enters into a transaction forming part of the scheme. The user must continue to include the scheme reference number for every subsequent year or period until the advantage ceases to apply.

162. The allocation of a scheme reference number does not indicate that a tax authority accepts the efficacy of the disclosed scheme or the completeness of a disclosure. Both the United States and United Kingdom are explicit in this regard. The US instructions make it clear that receipt of a reportable transaction number does not indicate that the IRS has reviewed, examined or approved the transaction. The UK guidance also states that the allocation or notification of a scheme reference number does not indicate that the UK tax administration accepts that the scheme achieves, or is capable of achieving, any purported tax advantage. Nor does it indicate acceptance that the disclosure is complete.

Box 2.9. **Options for identifying scheme users**

- Option A: Through scheme number and clients list
- Option B: Through clients list only

Option A: Through scheme number and clients list

163. The United States, the United Kingdom and Canada use a scheme reference number as a unique identifier for different schemes.[11] Promoters or material advisors receive a number for the disclosed scheme or transaction which they provide to taxpayers who have implemented the scheme. Taxpayers must include the scheme number on their tax returns on which the transaction is disclosed. In addition, the United Kingdom require promoters to provide a quarterly report of clients to the tax authority and the US material advisor must maintain a list of clients and furnish the list (together with all documents that are relevant to determining the tax treatment of the transaction) to the IRS within 20 business days after the date of a written request by the IRS.

164. Canada first introduced a TS regime in 1989 with a relatively narrow range of reportable transactions. Under the TS regime, a promoter is required to obtain a tax shelter identification number, provide the number to participants and provide the list of scheme users. The identification number allows the tax authorities to track the arrangement and taxpayers who participate in it. Canada has additionally introduced a new RTAT regime that extends disclosure to avoidance schemes that were not caught under the TS regime. However the scheme reference number only applies to tax shelters under the TS regime and does not apply to reportable transactions under RTAT.

165. Using a combination of a scheme reference number and a client list can help a tax authority to more easily identify the extent to which a scheme has been used and should ensure that there is full disclosure. Scheme reference numbers may also enable a tax authority to identify an individual taxpayer's appetite for undertaking certain types of transactions, as a tax administration can quickly and easily see what schemes the taxpayer has been involved in. This can then inform the risk assessment process for that particular taxpayer. However there may be higher up front resource and compliance costs from using a scheme reference number.

Option B: Through clients list only

166. Client lists can provide an alternative for user identification if countries do not use a scheme reference number system. Under such a requirement a promoter is obliged to provide the tax administration with a list of clients who have used a scheme. The time limits for providing client lists vary. Under the old Irish regime the list must be provided within 30-days of the promoter first becoming aware of any transaction forming part of the reportable transaction having been implemented without assigning any unique scheme number to the transaction. However Ireland introduced scheme reference numbers in 2014 and now has a similar system to the UK system.[12] On the other hand the United Kingdom requires the promoter to provide lists quarterly.[13]

167. A variation of this approach is to require the promoter to maintain lists identifying each person to whom a promoter has provided a scheme reference number with the promoter furnishing a list, upon request, to the tax authority. For example, the United States requires clients list to be provided to the IRS within 20 business days after the date of a written request by the IRS.

Further considerations

168. As mentioned above identification of users is an essential part of a mandatory disclosure regime. It allows a tax administration to improve risk assessment and the targeting of enquiries; it also enables them to better quantify the extent of any revenue loss.

All scheme details are filed per that scheme reference number, facilitating the easy retrieval of the details at a later date if required. Where a user is required to disclose directly to the tax administration, as is the case in the United States, then there is less of a need to include a further requirement, such as a scheme reference number, to identify a user, but gathering information from multiple sources (although it does use more resources) also allows for double-checking and easier linking between the promoter and the participants in the transaction. Requiring that the promoter provide a list may also identify other taxpayers that participated in a scheme but did not disclose.

169. However where the primary disclosure obligation is placed on the promoter, other mechanisms need to be introduced to ensure that users of the scheme can be identified. Countries may need to undertake data analysis on the basis of tax returns in order to identify scheme users if they do not have comprehensive information on the scheme users through the operation of scheme number systems or client lists. In addition, in this second situation, the fact that the user knows they will be identified either through a client list or more directly, through entering a number on their tax return, may deter some from undertaking a scheme in the first place. In conclusion, different considerations arise where there is a dual-reporting requirement compared to those that arise where only the promoter discloses. In this second situation there appears to be a much greater need for scheme reference numbers and client lists.

170. Using a scheme reference number may initially increase both the resource costs for the tax administration and the compliance costs for the promoter. However, once a process has been set up it seems likely that the on-going costs would be low. Balanced against this a tax administration not only obtains information on the users of a specific scheme it can also build up a picture of the risk presented by individual taxpayers. The use of scheme reference numbers may also improve administrative processes for instance, in South Africa; a scheme reference number is issued as a control measure to indicate the date and the sequence of the reporting. There may also be a greater deterrent effect if a taxpayer is personally obliged to include a scheme reference number on their returns, obviously the same deterrent effect arises if the taxpayer has an obligation to make a disclosure directly.

171. Client lists are generally received before a tax return so they provide information about the uptake of avoidance schemes much earlier than scheme reference numbers alone. This allows compliance plans to be put in place before tax returns are received, sometimes a year in advance. It also enables a tax authority to carry out early interventions such as contacting taxpayers who appear on the lists to advise them not to claim the effects of the avoidance scheme on their returns. These benefits are likely to be more obvious if client lists are automatically provided to the tax administration and the lists are provided sooner rather than later. However not all countries' domestic laws may enable automatic provision so there needs to be some flexibility.

Recommendations

172. Where a country places the primary reporting obligation on the promoter it is recommended that they introduce scheme reference numbers and require the preparation of client lists in order to fully identify all users of a scheme and to enable risk assessment of individual taxpayers. In this context it is recommended that, where domestic law allows, client lists should automatically be provided to the tax administration.

173. Where a country introduces a dual-reporting obligation where both the promoter and the taxpayer report then scheme reference numbers and clients lists may not be as essential

however they are likely to aid cross-checking and allow a tax administration to quantify the risk and tax loss from specific schemes.

Consequences of compliance and non-compliance

Consequences of compliance

Legitimate expectation

174. Disclosure of a reportable transaction enables a tax authority to identify a transaction of potential interest to them as well as the taxpayer seeking to obtain a tax benefit from that transaction. Generally the fact that a transaction is reportable does not necessarily mean that it involves tax avoidance. Equally disclosure does not imply any acceptance of the validity, or tax treatment, of the transaction by the tax authority.

175. Several countries have expressed concern about 'legitimate expectations' in the context of a mandatory disclosure regime. That is, they are concerned that where an obligation to disclose is introduced taxpayers may believe that any disclosure to the tax authorities leads to an implicit agreement that the scheme is valid, if there is no response to the contrary from the tax authority. If such a legitimate expectation were to arise it could impact on a tax authority's ability to subsequently act against a scheme and a requirement to respond to all disclosures would effectively provide a clearance mechanism for such transactions. This would be contrary to the existing practice of many countries who explicitly exclude avoidance transactions from their clearance or rulings process.

176. To avoid legitimate expectations from arising it is important for tax authorities to be clear that the disclosure of reportable transactions has nothing to do with the effectiveness of the transactions nor is there any automatic link to obtaining a ruling on the validity of the transaction or to the application of any anti-avoidance rules. Existing regimes already do this with the United Kingdom, United States, Ireland and Canada making it clear that the mere reporting of any scheme does not have any bearing on whether or not a tax benefit is allowed. Similarly it is clear that the disclosure of a tax arrangement has no effect on the tax position of any person who uses the tax arrangement.

177. The Portuguese regime operates within a civil law system but as with the regimes in operation in the United Kingdom, the United States, Ireland and South Africa, the disclosure of the scheme does not affect how it is treated and the lack of response from the tax authority does not give rise to a legitimate expectation, on the part of the taxpayer, that the scheme is valid or will be accepted.

178. It is therefore recommended that when introducing a mandatory disclosure regime the legislation and guidance follows the approach adopted in existing regimes and makes it clear that the disclosure of a transaction does not imply any acceptance of that transaction or any acceptance of the purported tax benefit obtained by any person.

Issue of self-incrimination

179. The information that a taxpayer is required to provide under a mandatory disclosure regime is generally no greater than the information that the tax administration could require under an investigation or audit into a tax return. Potential tax avoidance and tax planning transactions reported under existing mandatory disclosure regimes should not therefore give rise to any greater concern over self-incrimination than would arise under the exercise of other information collection powers. Furthermore the types of transactions

targeted for disclosure will not generally be the types of transactions that will give rise to criminal liabilities. For countries that impose criminal liabilities on taxpayers for undertaking certain tax avoidance transactions, it may be possible to simply exclude those transactions from the scope of the disclosure regime without substantially curtailing the scope of the regime. In addition there should not be an issue with self-incrimination where a promoter is obliged to disclose instead of a taxpayer except in the circumstances where the promoter could have criminal liability in relation to the promotion or facilitation of a scheme. Further details on the compatibility between self-incrimination and mandatory disclosure are included in Annex B.

Consequences of non-compliance

180. Mandatory disclosure regimes will not be effective unless promoters and taxpayers fully comply with the reporting requirement. Compliance with disclosure requirements can be enhanced in several ways; first of all rules that are precisely articulated and clearly understood will be easier to comply with; second mandatory disclosure regimes need to include clear sanctions to encourage disclosure and to penalise those who do not fulfil their obligations. The usual sanction for non-disclosure is the imposition of penalties but the structure and amount of the penalty varies among countries depending on the type of taxpayer (i.e. corporate or individual) and the type of transaction.

181. The question of whether penalties should be monetary, non-monetary or include elements of both, and the amounts of any monetary penalties will generally be an issue for each country to consider. However, the following discussion looks at the issues that will need to be taken into account, based on the provisions in existing regimes.

Monetary penalties

182. Non-compliance with mandatory disclosure rules and therefore monetary penalties could arise in a number of situations:

- *Monetary penalty for non-disclosure of a scheme* – this is the most common type of penalty and will arise where the promoter or the taxpayer fail to disclose a transaction or fail to report complete information.
- *Monetary penalty for failure to provide or maintain client lists* – a penalty may also be imposed if the promoter is required to provide or maintain a client list and he fails to comply with the obligation.
- *Monetary penalty for failure to provide a scheme reference number* – penalties may arise if a promoter is required to provide a scheme reference number to all relevant clients and fails to do so, or fails to do so within a specified time frame.
- *Monetary penalty for failure to report a scheme reference number* – a penalty may also be applied to a taxpayer if he is required to report a scheme reference number on his return but he fails to do so.

The structure of penalties for non-disclosure

183. In setting penalty levels jurisdictions may take into account factors such as whether there is negligence or deliberate non-compliance or penalties may be linked to the level of fees or tax benefit. However, the main aim in setting a limit and in fixing a penalty structure is to increase the pressure to comply with the law. Penalties should be set at

a level that encourages compliance and maximises their deterrent value without being overly burdensome or disproportionate. Consideration should be given to percentage based penalties based upon transaction size or the extent of any tax savings.

(i) Daily penalties

184. Daily penalties put an emphasis on timely disclosure and are used in the United Kingdom and Ireland. They may be effective in encouraging the promoter and taxpayer to comply with the disclosure obligation as further daily penalties can be imposed if non-compliance continues. Under the UK regime, penalties consist of two types: an initial penalty and a secondary penalty. The initial penalty is determined by a Tribunal and a secondary daily penalty may be imposed by the UK tax administration. The initial penalty may be calculated on the basis of a daily amount not exceeding GBP 600 a day.[14]

185. If the Tribunal considers that the maximum daily penalty described above is likely to be insufficient it may determine a higher penalty of up to GBP 1 million. The higher penalty amount is determined having regard to the amount of fees received or likely to have been received by the promoter, in the case of non-compliance by a promoter. In the case of a failure to disclose by the taxpayer, the Tribunal will have regard to the amount of the tax advantage gained or sought to be gained.

186. In addition, the UK tax administration may impose a secondary daily penalty, not exceeding GBP 600, for each day that the failure to disclose continues after an initial penalty has been imposed. In such cases, the UK tax administration normally imposes a secondary daily amount that is proportionate to the initial penalty. So the penalty structure used in the United Kingdom and Ireland do also take account of the amount of tax benefit or fees received.

187. However a different approach is taken if a user fails to report the use of a scheme on a return. In this situation the penalties are GBP 100 for the first failure, GBP 500 for a second failure and GBP 1 000 for any subsequent failures. Ireland has a similar penalties regime to that of the United Kingdom although the monetary amounts differ.

188. Daily penalties can be also imposed on any promoter or advisor who fails to maintain a client list and to make that available upon request. For instance under US tax law, any material advisor who fails to maintain a list under the reportable transaction regime, and who fails to provide the list to the IRS upon written request shall pay a penalty of USD 10 000 per day for each day of failure after the 20th day.

(ii) Penalty proportionate to tax savings or promoter's fee

189. The penalty structure used by the United Kingdom and Ireland can take into account the amount of the tax benefit or the fees received. However the approach taken by the United States and Canada makes this link more explicitly by directly basing the level of penalties on the amount of the tax benefit achieved by the taxpayer or on the fees/remuneration paid to the advisor or promoter.

190. In the United States, the penalty for a material advisor failing to disclose a reportable transaction other than a listed transaction, or for filing false or incomplete information with respect to such a transaction, is USD 50 000. The penalty imposed for listed transactions is the greater of USD 200 000 or 50% (increased to 75% where such failure or false or incomplete filing is intentional) of the gross income derived from providing aid, assistance, or advice with respect to the listed transaction.

191. For a US taxpayer, the penalty for taxpayer non-disclosure is 75% of the decrease in tax as a result of the transaction, subject to minimum and maximum penalties that range from USD 5 000 to USD 200 000 depending on the type of taxpayer and type of reportable transaction. These penalty amounts reflect changes made to the US penalty regime in 2010 to ensure that the penalty amount was proportionate to the misconduct being penalised.[15]

192. Under the Canadian penalty regime the penalty is proportionate to the amount of fees. Each person required to file is liable to pay a penalty equal to the total of all fees payable to the advisor or promoter. Each advisor or promoter is jointly and severally liable with the taxpayer, which incentivises advisors and promoters to report or to encourage their clients to report. However, advisors and promoters are liable only to the extent of fees that they are entitled to receive. This penalty is not explicitly linked to the tax benefits received by the user, however, it will implicitly reflect the benefits to the extent that the fees are based on the tax benefit received.

193. In South Africa, a monthly penalty for non-disclosure of between ZAR 50 000 and ZAR 100 000 (for up to 12 months) is imposed and the penalty is doubled if the amount of the anticipated tax benefit exceeds ZAR 5 million and is tripled if the anticipated tax benefit exceeds ZAR 10 million.

194. Penalties for failure to comply with a disclosure regime generally relate to the disclosure itself not the tax consequences of the underlying scheme. Disclosure penalties therefore, operate separately to, and are independent of, other penalty provisions in a country's domestic tax code and the disclosure of a scheme cannot cure a separate failure to comply with some other aspect of a taxpayer's obligations. Some examples, based on the provisions of the United Kingdom and the United States are included in Annex C.

Non-monetary penalties

195. Non-monetary penalties can also be applied. For instance, a failure to disclose suspends the efficacy of the scheme and taxpayers can be denied any tax benefit arising from the scheme in Canada. On the other hand, non-disclosure itself does not affect the efficacy of a scheme in the United States, the United Kingdom, Portugal, Ireland and South Africa.

196. In the United States, publicly traded companies that are required to file certain reports with the Securities and Exchange Commission (SEC) are required to disclose the requirement to pay the monetary penalty for failure to disclose certain reportable transactions. In the United States, the failure to comply with the disclosure rules may also impact on whether the taxpayer is able to mount an effective defence to any penalty for a substantive tax understatement relating to the transaction (i.e. the non-disclosure may impact on the analysis of whether the taxpayer acted with "reasonable cause and good faith" in taking the tax-reporting position). Additionally in the United States, non-disclosure extends the statute of limitations (the time period the government has to dispute a taxpayer's claimed tax treatment) in respect of listed transactions.

Initiatives targeting promoters

197. Promoters have a greater knowledge of a scheme's tax effects and are better placed to know whether a scheme constitutes tax avoidance and to be aware of any risks inherent in that scheme. For this reason tax compliance strategies, including mandatory disclosure rules, are likely to be more effective if they focus on promoters, and improving tax compliance via the supply side, rather than focusing exclusively on the end user, i.e. the taxpayer. This

dual approach is evident outside the context of mandatory disclosure regimes for instance under the Mexican tax code a penalty is imposed on a tax advisor who provides an advisory service to a taxpayer in order to reduce or omit some federal contribution. However this penalty is not applicable if the tax advisor provides the taxpayer with a written opinion saying that the tax authority may not agree with the position taken. This type of penalty regime encourages the tax advisor to advise his clients of the risk of undertaking certain transactions and may also, more generally, encourage a tax advisor to be more careful about the advice he provides.

198. Other promoter initiatives may also be considered as part of, or in connection with a mandatory disclosure regime. For instance the United Kingdom tackles the behaviour of high-risk promoters in order to increase transparency and is introducing new rules. The rules make a promoter who fails to comply with the disclosure regime vulnerable to further action by the tax authority, including information powers and penalties, designed to improve their behaviour. In its consultation document entitled "Strengthening the Tax Avoidance Disclosure Regimes" published in July 2014,[16] the UK tax administration suggests that anyone working with a non-resident promoter (such as a business partner) should be required to disclose reportable arrangements that are promoted by the offshore promoter to deter the use of offshore promoters to circumvent the UK disclosure requirements.

Recommendations

199. It is recommended that countries are explicit in their domestic law about the consequences of reporting a scheme or transaction under a disclosure regime, i.e. that this does not imply acceptance of the scheme or its purported benefits.

200. In order to enforce compliance with mandatory disclosure rules, countries should introduce financial penalties that apply if there is failure to comply with any of the obligations introduced. Countries are free to introduce penalty provisions (including non-monetary penalties) that are coherent with their general domestic law provisions.

Procedural/tax administration matters

Types of information to be reported

201. Once a transaction is reportable, the person who is obliged to disclose must provide the tax authorities with particular information about how the transaction works and how the expected tax benefit arises along with details of the promoter and scheme user. Commonly, the information to be reported is the kind of information that a taxpayer would need to comply with their tax obligations in any event and includes details of the transactions, names and the tax reference number for the promoter and scheme users.

202. Promoters and, in certain circumstances, users need to provide sufficient information to a tax authority to enable them to understand how a scheme operates and how the expected tax advantage arises. A possible draft template setting out the type of information required to be reported under existing mandatory disclosure regimes is set out below. This is based on the forms used in the mandatory disclosure regimes of the United Kingdom, the United States, Canada, Ireland and South Africa.[17]

Identification of promoters and scheme users

203. To identify the promoters and scheme users, details including the full name, address, phone number and tax reference or identification number (if any) are required. In Canada and South Africa there is a single form available for use by a scheme user and a promoter. Other countries (the United Kingdom, the United States and Ireland) require the promoter and taxpayer to use a separate form for disclosure.

Details of the provision that makes the scheme reportable

204. Promoters or scheme users are required to specify the provision, i.e. the hallmark(s), under which the disclosure is being made. Where more than one hallmark applies, the United States, Canada, Ireland and South Africa require them to specify all hallmarks that apply to the reportable transaction. The United Kingdom, however, only requires a promoter or scheme user to indicate the main hallmark that is applicable (this allows the UK tax administration to monitor the effectiveness of the different hallmarks).

Description of the arrangements and the name by which they are known (if any)

205. Sufficient information must be provided to enable a tax authority to understand how the expected tax advantage arises. The explanation should be clear and describe each step involved. Common technical or legal terms and concepts need not be explained in depth but the description of the reportable transaction/s must include the relevant facts, details of the parties involved, full details of each element of the transaction and must explain how the expected tax advantage arises.

Statutory provisions on which tax advantage is based.

206. There should be a full reference to the legislative and regulatory provisions relevant to the tax treatment of the transactions. This information explains how the relevant provisions are being applied and how they allow the taxpayer to obtain the desired tax treatment. In the context of international tax schemes such information should include relevant provisions of foreign law.

Description of tax benefit or advantage

207. The promoter and/or the taxpayer are required to describe the tax advantage generated by the arrangements. In the United States, the taxpayer must check all the boxes that apply to the tax benefits expected from the transaction. In other countries the taxpayer has to describe the tax advantages.

List of clients (promoter only)

208. Certain mandatory disclosure regimes require promoters and tax advisors to provide client lists at the time of disclosure or, in the case of the United States, promoters are required to maintain a client list and provide it upon request.

Amount of expected tax benefit

209. Some countries (the United States, Canada and South Africa) require the actual or expected amount of the tax benefit generated by the disclosed scheme to be reflected on the disclosure form. For example, in the United States, each taxpayer and material advisor is required to report a reportable transaction on a separate form. To be considered complete, a taxpayer must report the amounts of the expected tax treatment and all the potential tax benefits expected to result from the transaction. However, it may be difficult for a taxpayer to accurately calculate the amount of a tax benefit and this is particularly likely where the disclosure obligation arises before a scheme is implemented (i.e. when a scheme is made available by a promoter) for this reason this information is described as optional in Boxes 2.10 and 2.11.

Box 2.10. **Draft disclosure form A (for scheme user)**

- **User's details** : name, address, phone number, tax reference number *(if any)*
- **Scheme details**: describe each element in the transaction from which the intended tax effect arises
- **Disclosure provision**: specify relevant hallmark(s) under which the disclosure is being made
- **Statutory or regulatory provisions**: describe the key provisions of law relevant to the elements of the disclosed transaction from which the expected tax benefit arises
- **Amount of expected tax benefit** *(optional)*
- **Details of all parties to the transaction**: useful particularly where bespoke schemes are being reported
- **Declaration**: signature, date, name of signatory

Box 2.11. **Draft disclosure form B (for scheme promoter or advisor)**

- **Promoter or advisor's details** : name, address, phone number, tax reference number *(if any)*
- **Scheme details**: describe each element in the transaction from which the intended tax effect arises
- **Disclosure provisions**: specify relevant hallmark(s) under which the disclosure is being made
- **Statutory or regulatory provisions**: describe the key provisions of law relevant to the elements of the disclosed transaction from which the expected tax benefit arises
- **List of clients:** name of clients to whom the transaction was offered (where domestic law allows)
- **Amount of expected tax benefit** *(optional)*
- **Details of all parties to the transaction** : useful particularly where bespoke schemes are being reported
- **Declaration**: signature, date, name of signatory

Powers to obtain additional information

210. Once an initial disclosure has been received a tax administration may need to follow this up with a request for additional information, for instance to obtain further details about a scheme and how it operates or to clarify information that is incomplete or unclear. In addition information powers may also be necessary where no disclosure has actually been made, to check that the taxpayer and promoter are complying with their disclosure obligations.

211. Consideration will therefore need to be given to the extent to which new or additional powers are necessary to enable a tax administration to:

- enquire into the reasons why a scheme has not been disclosed by a promoter or a user in circumstances where it believes a disclosure should have been made;
- require an intermediary/introducer (a person who introduces clients to a promoter) to identify the person who provided them with information relating to the scheme;[18]
- call for more information where a disclosure is incomplete;
- request further information, after an initial disclosure from the promoter or user of a proposal or arrangement.

Use of the information collected

212. Once a mandatory disclosure regime is introduced there are several ways in which tax authorities can use the information collected to change behaviour and to counteract tax avoidance schemes. These include counteraction through legislative change; through risk assessment and audit; and through communication strategies.

Legislative or regulatory change

213. The early detection of tax avoidance schemes enables tax authorities to make changes to tax law more quickly. For example, in the United Kingdom, there have been numerous changes in tax law, informed by disclosures, since DOTAS was introduced in 2004. This has helped to close off billions in avoidance opportunities.

214. Quick legislative change is dependent on a country's legislative system but also requires a country to set up a process that analyses and risk assesses new schemes quickly.

Risk assessment

215. There is generally a dedicated team, within the tax administration, dealing with disclosures. This team undertakes an initial review of the arrangement and plays a role in determining whether further action should be taken in the form of legislative change, audits, or more inquiries, etc. The specific internal procedure varies depending on the administrative structure of countries.

216. In the United Kingdom, once a disclosure is received, a separate team assesses the risk of the disclosed arrangement and co-ordinates responses from different policy and operational areas. This includes devising and delivering the operational strategy for handling enquiries into the respective avoidance scheme. In the United States, a team called the Office of Tax Shelter Analysis (OTSA) is the focal point for tax shelter compliance, responsible for monitoring all reportable transactions disclosed and for

identifying potential cases of non-compliance, and ensuring the appropriate dissemination of tax shelter information within the tax administration.

Communication strategy

217. Tax authorities may issue publications to taxpayers as a way of providing an early warning that they have detected an arrangement in the marketplace and are currently considering its tax implications. In such publications tax authorities describe the arrangement and their concerns with the arrangement so that taxpayers are aware of the risks in undertaking the scheme. This mass media ("one too many") approach can play an important role in influencing taxpayer's and promoter's behaviour on tax compliance. For instance the United Kingdom issues 'Spotlight' which warns taxpayers about certain tax avoidance schemes.[19]

218. Canada has a product similar to the United Kingdom, which is called 'Tax Alert'.[20] The CRA occasionally issues 'Tax Alert' on specific tax issues in order to help tax payers understand the tax consequences they might face if they undertake a scheme or transaction. These publications are a way of providing timely communication to taxpayers to keep them informed and to potentially deter them from undertaking certain transactions.

219. In the United States, the IRS publicises its view of transactions that it has identified as tax avoidance transactions by designating such transactions as "listed transactions" in administrative notices or other public guidance.[21] The IRS also identifies transactions that it has determined may have the potential for tax avoidance by designating such transactions as "transactions of interest" in administrative notices or other public guidance.[22] These public notices describe both the features of identified transactions and their intended tax effects.

Recommendations

220. Tax administrations will need to set out the information that a promoter or taxpayer is required to disclose. It is recommended that the information should include:

- identification of promoters and scheme users;
- details of the provisions that make the scheme reportable;
- a description of the arrangements and the name by which they are known (if any);
- details of the statutory provisions on which a tax advantage is based;
- a description of the tax benefit or advantage;
- a list of clients (promoter only) – where domestic law allows;
- the amount of expected tax benefit.

221. In addition any mandatory disclosure provisions will need to be supported by information powers necessary to enable a tax administration to:

- enquire into the reasons for a failure to disclose;
- enquire into the identity of promoters and intermediaries;
- request further follow up information in response to a disclosure.

222. In order to use the information from a mandatory disclosure regime effectively it is recommended that tax administrations set up a small unit to risk assess the disclosures received and to co-ordinate action within and across the taxing authorities.

Notes

1. Hallmarks act as tools to identify the features of aggressive tax planning schemes and are generally divided into two categories: generic and specific hallmarks. Further details are included in section "Hallmarks" in this chapter.

2. Except for those cases where litigation is in actual contemplation, legal privilege generally only applies to confidential legal advice given to the client by the professional adviser and does not extend to documentation prepared in the ordinary course of the transaction or to the identity of the parties involved. The legal professional privilege is similar to the attorney-client privilege recognised under US common law. US legislation also recognises a statutory protection for communications between a taxpayer and a practitioner authorised to practice before the IRS, but like the attorney privilege, this generally does not extend to the identity of the taxpayer. *See,* e.g. *United States v. BDO Seidman*, 337 F.3d 802 (7th Cir. 2003); *Doe v. KPMG LLP*, 325 F. Supp. 2d 746 (N.D. Tex. 2004). Furthermore, the US statutory protection does not protect communications regarding tax shelters.

3. Thresholds test are used in a number of different legislative provisions and often refer to de-minimis limits. However, in the context of existing mandatory disclosure regimes, the most common threshold is a main benefit or main purpose test. Therefore when this report refers to threshold tests this is the type of test that is being referred to.

4. However, as mentioned earlier, the experience of some countries indicates that the introduction of generic hallmarks reduces the prevalence of certain transactions so further thresholds may not be necessary.

5. See HMRC (2014), *Disclosure of Tax Avoidance Schemes: Guidance*, 14 May 2014, p. 40.

6. See HMRC (2014), *Disclosure of Tax Avoidance Schemes: Guidance*, 14 May 2014, p. 46.

7. Canada has two kinds of mandatory disclosure regimes: tax shelter (TS) regime, reporting of tax avoidance transactions (RTAT). The TS regime which was introduced in 1989 is narrow in scope as it includes only gifting arrangements and the acquisition of property. As such, while it has been effective in providing timely information, many more tax avoidance arrangements are not caught by the rule. The new mandatory disclosure regime, which was enacted in 2013, is intended to disclose tax avoidance arrangements not caught under the tax shelter regime.

8. For more details, see Notice 2006-6, 2006-5 I.R.B. 385: www.irs.gov/pub/irs-irbs/irb06-05.pdf (accessed 17 June 2015).

9. It could also be the case that the taxpayer ultimately decides not to claim the aggressive or abusive tax benefits on the return.

10. Scheme reference numbers may have less importance where there is a dual reporting requirement imposed on both the promoter and taxpayer such as in the United States. The fact that both taxpayers and promoters/material advisors report in the United States may also reduce the reliance on client lists. Scheme reference numbers and client lists would appear to be more essential in the context of a regime that places the primary reporting obligation on the promoter and only requires the user to report in limited circumstances. One additional benefit to dual reporting is the ability to cross-check.

11. Under the South African mandatory disclosure regime, a reference number is issued to taxpayers, who must disclose that they entered into a reportable transaction and include the reference number in their annual tax returns. However, the South African regime does not use a client list.

12. Any disclosable transaction which is commenced after 23 October 2014 must be assigned a unique transaction number by the Irish Revenue (Chapter 3 of Part 33 of the Taxes Consolidation Act (as amended by Finance Act 2014)).

13. Note that legal privilege generally does not extend to client lists.

14. "Initial period" begins with the first day following the end of the period in which the scheme should have been disclosed and ends with the earlier of: the day on which the Tribunal determines the penalty or the last day before the day on which the scheme is disclosed.

15. The 2010 amendment to the penalty regime apply to penalties assessed after December 31, 2006. Prior to the amendment, a taxpayer that failed to disclose a listed transaction was subject to a flat penalty of USD 100 000 in the case of an individual, or USD 200 000 in any other case. A taxpayer that failed to disclose a reportable transaction that was not a listed transaction was subject to a flat penalty of USD 10 000 in the case of an individual, or USD 50 000 in any other case.

16. https://www.gov.uk/government/consultations/strengthening-the-tax-avoidance-disclosure-regimes (accessed 14 June 2015).

17. Links to disclosure forms available at:
    - UK: https://www.gov.uk/forms-to-disclose-tax-avoidance-schemes (accessed 17 June 2015)
        - US: www.irs.gov/pub/irs-pdf/f8918.pdf, www.irs.gov/pub/irs-pdf/f8886.pdf (accessed 17 June 2015)
        - Ireland: www.revenue.ie/en/practitioner/law/mandatory-disclosure.html (accessed 17 June 2015)
        - South Africa: www.sars.gov.za/AllDocs/OpsDocs/SARSForms/RA01%20-%20Reporting%20Reportable%20Arrangements%20-%20External%20Form.pdf (accessed 17 June 2015)
        - Canada: www.cra-arc.gc.ca/E/pbg/tf/rc312/rc312-13e.pdf, www.cra-arc.gc.ca/E/pbg/tf/t5001/t5001-14e.pdf (accessed 17 June 2015).

18. The United Kingdom has such a provision which applies where they suspect a person of acting as an introducer for a notifiable scheme that has not been disclosed.

19. Spotlight, available at: https://www.gov.uk/government/publications/tax-avoidance-schemes-currently-in-the-spotlight (accessed 17 June 2015).

20. Tax Alert, available at: www.cra-arc.gc.ca/nwsrm/lrts/menu-eng.html (accessed 17 June 2015).

21. An up-to-date record of listed transactions is available at: www.irs.gov/Businesses/Corporations/Listed-Transactions (accessed 17 June 2015).

22. Links to transactions of interest available at: www.irs.gov/Businesses/Corporations/Transactions-of-Interest---Not-LMSB-Tier-I-Issues (accessed 17 June 2015).

Bibliography

HMRC (2014), *Disclosure of Tax Avoidance Schemes: Guidance*, 14 May 2014 https://www.gov.uk/government/uploads/system/uploads/attachment_data/file/341960/dotas-guidance.pdf (accessed 17 June 2015).

Irish Revenue Commissioners (2011), Guidance Notes on Mandatory Disclosure Regime, January 2015, www.revenue.ie/en/practitioner/law/notes-for-guidance/mandatory-disclosure/ (accessed 17 June 2015).

Chapter 3

International tax schemes

223. Part of the work required under Action 12 is considering how to make mandatory disclosure more effective in the international context. Action 12 specifically calls for recommendations on the mandatory disclosure of international tax schemes and the exploration of a wide definition of "tax benefit" in order to capture them.

224. The work under Action 12 is intended to give countries an additional tool for tackling BEPS by providing tax administrations with real-time information on cross-border tax planning. As noted in Chapter 1, one of the key strengths of mandatory disclosure is its ability to provide tax administrations with current, comprehensive and relevant information on actual taxpayer behaviour. These benefits are particularly important in the context of cross-border schemes where tax administrations could otherwise find it difficult to obtain information on the facts of a scheme or a complete picture of its overall tax and economic consequences. The challenge, however, is to develop disclosure requirements that are appropriately targeted and that capture the key information tax administrations need in order to make informed policy decisions, while avoiding over-disclosure or placing undue compliance burdens on taxpayers.

225. This chapter identifies some of the key differences between domestic and international schemes that make such schemes more difficult to tackle from a disclosure perspective. It then sets out recommendations for elements that could be included in mandatory disclosure regimes to make them more effective at targeting cross-border tax planning.

Application of existing disclosure rules

Defining a reportable scheme

226. There is nothing in principle that prevents current mandatory disclosure regimes from applying to international schemes. Existing disclosure regimes require any scheme to be disclosed if it meets any threshold requirement and the particular features of that scheme fall within one of the hallmarks. The existing hallmarks used in mandatory disclosure regimes do not generally discriminate between schemes that are wholly domestic and those that have a cross-border component and some jurisdictions also have hallmarks that specifically target cross-border schemes or may separately identify an international transaction under their rules.

227. Several countries with mandatory disclosure regimes indicate, however, that, in practice, they receive comparatively fewer disclosures of cross-border schemes. The reason for this lower number of disclosures appears to be partly a consequence of the way international schemes are structured and the approach taken by these regimes in formulating the requirements for disclosure of a reportable scheme.

228. Cross-border schemes typically generate multiple tax benefits for different parties in different jurisdictions and the domestic tax benefits that arise under a cross-border scheme may seem unremarkable when viewed in isolation from the rest of the arrangement as a whole. The ambiguous nature of the tax benefits that arise in respect of cross-border tax planning means that disclosure regimes which focus exclusively on domestic tax outcomes for domestic taxpayers, without understanding the global picture, may not capture many types of cross-border tax planning.

229. As discussed in Chapter 2, some disclosure regimes require reportable schemes to meet a formal threshold condition for disclosure (such as the *main benefit* or *tax avoidance* test). This threshold condition can be difficult to apply in the context of cross-border schemes that trigger tax consequences in a number of different jurisdictions. Such schemes may not meet

the disclosure threshold if the taxpayer can demonstrate that the value of any domestic tax benefits was incidental when viewed in light of the commercial and foreign tax benefits of the transaction as a whole. In certain cases the foreign tax benefits of a cross-border scheme may even be returned to the taxpayer in the reporting jurisdiction in the form of a lower cost of capital or higher return. This has the effect of converting a tax benefit for a foreign counterparty in the off-shore jurisdiction into a commercial benefit for the taxpayer in the reporting jurisdiction, thereby further reducing the overall significance of the domestic tax benefits under the transaction that nevertheless may pose a risk to the domestic tax administration.

230. Cross-border tax planning schemes are often incorporated into a broader commercial transaction such as an acquisition, refinancing or restructuring. Such schemes tend to be customised so that they are taxpayer and transaction specific and may not be widely promoted in the same way as a domestically marketed scheme. It may therefore be difficult to target these schemes with generic hallmarks that target promoted schemes, which can be easily replicated and sold to a number of different taxpayers. Some countries target these more specialised types of tax planning with the use of broader generic hallmarks, such as the hypothetical premium fee test used in the United Kingdom and Ireland, which covers arrangements where the tax planning is sufficiently innovative that a promoter *would be able* to obtain a premium fee for it. These countries, however, typically limit the application of those hallmarks with a threshold condition that restricts the application to schemes that are designed with the main purpose of generating domestic tax benefits.

231. Specific hallmarks will generally be the most effective method of targeting cross-border tax schemes that raise tax policy or revenue risks in the reporting jurisdiction. Some of the specific hallmarks presently used in mandatory disclosure regimes (e.g. leasing, income conversion schemes) can apply equally in the domestic and cross-border context. Furthermore countries such as the United States, South Africa and Portugal have also developed specific hallmarks for targeting international transactions.

232. One of the challenges in the design of specific hallmarks is to formulate a definition that is sufficiently broad to pick up a range of tax planning techniques and narrow enough to avoid over-disclosure. One approach to dealing with this issue is to focus on the kinds of BEPS *outcomes* that raise concerns from a tax policy perspective, rather than the mechanisms that are used to achieve them. Identifying an international scheme by reference to a specific outcome and the general technique used to achieve it is similar to the US approach of extending the disclosure obligations to transactions that are "substantially similar" to listed transactions (i.e. transactions that are expected to achieve the same or similar consequences as a listed transaction and are based on the same or similar strategy).

Identifying who must report

233. A reporting jurisdiction should only require disclosure of an international scheme where the scheme has a substantive connection with the reporting jurisdiction (i.e. the scheme results in domestic tax consequences for a domestic taxpayer). A mandatory disclosure regime should avoid imposing disclosure obligations on persons that are not subject to tax in the reporting jurisdiction or on advisers or intermediaries that do not provide any advice or assistance in respect of domestic taxpayers or transactions. This means that a mandatory disclosure regime should only apply to domestic taxpayers and their advisors and only in respect of schemes that have a material impact on domestic tax outcomes in the reporting jurisdiction. Limiting disclosure in this way ensures that reporting obligations are not imposed in circumstances where the tax authority would have limited practical ability to enforce them.

234. Once the ability to require disclosure is established, further consideration needs to be given to how a taxpayer in the reporting jurisdiction would comply with additional information requirements for international tax schemes. Simply because an international scheme results in domestic consequences for a taxpayer does not mean that the taxpayer will be aware of the offshore elements of the scheme or be in a position to properly understand its effects. At the same time, disclosure obligations should not be framed in such a way as to encourage a taxpayer to deliberately ignore the offshore aspects of a scheme simply to avoid disclosure.

Describing what must be reported

235. Once a disclosure obligation has been triggered there remains the question of what information needs to be disclosed. While taxpayers should only be required to disclose information that is within their knowledge, possession or control, they can be expected to request information on the operation and effect of an intra-group scheme from other group members.

Recommendation on an alternative approach to the design of a disclosure regime for international tax schemes

236. Based on the above discussion the following design elements are recommended in order for a mandatory disclosure regime to better target cross-border tax planning:

- the removal of the threshold condition for cross-border schemes;
- the development of hallmarks that focus on BEPS related risks posed by cross-border schemes and that are wide enough to capture different and innovative tax planning techniques (cross-border outcomes);
- a broad definition of reportable scheme that would include any arrangement that incorporates a material transaction with a domestic taxpayer and that gives rise to a cross-border outcome.
- avoid imposing undue burden on taxpayers or their advisers by requiring disclosure only in circumstances where the domestic taxpayer or their advisor could reasonably have been expected to be aware of the cross-border outcome under the arrangement;
- require the domestic taxpayer or their advisor to disclose to the tax administration any material information on the scheme that is within their knowledge, possession or control;
- impose an obligation on a domestic taxpayer at the time they enter into a material transaction with a group member to:
  - make reasonable enquiries as to whether the arrangement that gave rise to the transaction incorporates a cross-border outcome identified in a hallmark developed under paragraph (b) above;
  - notify the tax administration if:
    - the group member does not provide relevant information on the arrangement;
    - the information on the arrangement is inadequate or incomplete;
    - there is an unreasonable delay in providing such information.

A more detailed explanation setting out the key elements of this approach is set out below.

No threshold requirement

237. The function of a threshold requirement is to filter out irrelevant disclosures and reduce the compliance and administration burden by targeting only tax motivated transactions that are likely to pose the greatest tax policy and revenue risks.

238. The hallmarks for international schemes (discussed below) would, however, target only arrangements that produced cross-border outcomes, which were of particular concern to a tax administration and would only require disclosure of those arrangements in circumstances where they presented a material risk to the reporting jurisdiction from a tax revenue perspective. Provided the new hallmarks give a precise description of the types of tax outcomes that are of concern to the reporting jurisdiction's tax administration and the materiality thresholds are set at level that avoids over-disclosure, there should be no need to apply a threshold requirement to filter-out irrelevant or non-material disclosures.

New hallmarks based on identification of cross-border tax outcomes

239. The most direct way of targeting cross-border schemes is for the tax administration to develop hallmarks that focus on the kinds of base erosion and profit shifting techniques that are known to give rise to tax policy or revenue concerns (cross-border outcomes). Cross-border outcomes would include the types of structures identified in the BEPS Action Plan (OECD, 2013) (for example, hybrid mismatch and treaty shopping arrangements) and may include other cross-border tax outcomes that are known to pose material risks to the tax base of a reporting jurisdiction. These could include, for example:

- Arrangements that give rise to a conflict in ownership of an asset that results in taxpayers in different jurisdictions claiming tax relief for depreciation or amortisation in respect of the same asset or claiming relief from double taxation in respect of the same item of income.
- Deductible cross-border payments made to members of the same group that are not resident for tax purposes in any jurisdiction or that are resident in a jurisdiction that does not impose tax on income.
- Transactions that give rise to a deduction or equivalent relief resulting from a deemed or actual transfer of value for tax purposes, where that transaction is not treated as giving rise to tax consequences in the jurisdiction of the counterparty.
- Asset transfers where there is a material difference in the amount treated as payable in consideration for the asset.

240. The hallmarks for international schemes must be both *specific*, in that they should identify particular cross-border tax outcomes that raise concerns for the reporting jurisdiction, and *generic*, in that they should be defined by reference to their overall tax effects and be capable of capturing any arrangement designed to produce those effects regardless of how the arrangement is actually structured. This combination of specific and generic elements will allow tax administrations to target those international tax planning arrangements that raise the most significant tax policy or revenue concerns while still capturing novel or innovative schemes. In addition to setting out general descriptions of cross-border outcomes, the tax administration should provide a specific list of tax regimes and outcomes that are not required to be disclosed under the international hallmarks in order to avoid disclosure of arrangements that are known to the tax administration and are not thought to raise any particular tax policy issues.

241. As part of the work on monitoring the outputs from the BEPS project, countries may consider whether additional hallmarks are required to ensure that the outputs of the BEPS project are working as intended. This work could include development of model hallmarks, in order to minimise the additional compliance costs that would otherwise flow from different countries targeting the same cross-border scheme with overlapping disclosure obligations, each with its own definition and scope.

Broad definition of arrangement that includes offshore tax outcomes

242. The definition of a "reportable scheme" in the international context should capture any arrangement involving a domestic taxpayer if that arrangement includes a cross-border outcome. Domestic taxpayers should be under an obligation to disclose their participation in that arrangement even if they are not a direct party to that cross-border outcome. If disclosure was only required from taxpayers that were directly affected by a cross-border outcome, then tax planners could simply use intermediaries and back-to-back structures to avoid triggering domestic disclosure requirements. Equally, however, a reporting jurisdiction should not require disclosure of cross-border arrangements that do not raise any material tax revenue risks in that jurisdiction. Accordingly an arrangement that gives rise to a specified cross-border outcome should only be reportable if it involves a transaction or payment that has a material tax impact on the reporting jurisdiction.

Arrangement

243. The definition of *arrangement* should be sufficiently broad and robust to capture any scheme, plan or understanding; all the steps and transactions that form part of that arrangement and all the persons that are a party to, or affected by that arrangement. For example, in the context of a group financing (or re-financing), the arrangement would cover the initial transaction that introduced new capital into the group and all the subsequent steps and intra-group transactions that explain how the capital was deployed: including transactions taken in contemplation of, or as a consequence of, the financing or refinancing. In the context of the acquisition of a new entity, the arrangement would include not only the acquisition itself but also the financing of the acquisition and any post-acquisition restructuring. Although the definition of arrangement should be broadly construed, so as to pick up any arrangement incorporating a cross-border outcome that gives rise to material tax consequences in the reporting jurisdiction, it is only those transactions that explain the direct or indirect tax effects of the cross-border outcome in the reporting jurisdiction that should be required to be disclosed (see below).

Arrangement includes a cross-border outcome

244. Any arrangement that incorporates a specified cross-border outcome will potentially be subject to disclosure. A mandatory disclosure regime for international schemes should not limit disclosure to those schemes where the cross-border outcome is the purpose or one of the main purposes of the arrangement. It will be sufficient to bring an arrangement within the purview of a mandatory disclosure rule if the effect of the arrangements is to bring about a cross-border outcome, noting that the cross-border outcome itself will need to be set forth with a high degree of specificity so that taxpayer's can easily determine whether a transaction is in scope.

Arrangement includes a transaction with a material tax impact

245. The requirement that the arrangement includes a transaction with a *material tax impact* in the reporting jurisdiction ensures that international schemes are only reportable in those jurisdictions where they actually have tax revenue impacts.

246. An arrangement will have a tax impact on a reporting jurisdiction if the arrangement has the effect, or is likely to have the effect, of reducing the tax payable in that reporting jurisdiction. The tax impact should be material. The materiality threshold should be a monetary amount (to facilitate certainty) and set by reference to the economic and tax consequences of the transaction entered into by the domestic taxpayer (or payments made by or to that taxpayer). Materiality should be measured over the lifetime of the arrangement.

247. Measuring whether a transaction has a tax impact does not require a before-and-after comparison of the tax consequences of the transaction that has been entered into, but rather a direct analysis of the economic and tax impact of the transaction and any payments made under it. Transactions or payments with a tax impact could, for example, include a payment of interest to an offshore related party, a payment that is eligible for treaty relief or the transfer of an income-earning asset to a non-resident. The definition of transaction should also capture notional or deemed transactions that are recognised for tax purposes in the counterparty jurisdiction even if such transactions are not treated as having any economic or tax consequences in the reporting jurisdiction (such as a deemed transfer of goodwill).

Domestic taxpayer

248. A *domestic taxpayer*, in this context should include any person that is tax resident in the reporting jurisdiction and any non-resident to the extent that person is subject to a tax reporting obligation on income that has a source or nexus in the reporting jurisdiction.

Limitations on disclosure

249. In order to prevent mandatory disclosure imposing an undue burden on taxpayers, disclosure in the reporting jurisdiction should only be required where the taxpayer could reasonably have been expected to be aware of the cross-border outcome under the arrangement.

250. A person can reasonably be expected to be aware of a cross-border outcome where the person has sufficient information about the arrangement to understand its design and to appreciate its tax effects. This will include any information obtained by a taxpayer under the obligation to make reasonable enquiries (described below) but, in the context of transactions with unrelated parties, the test should not be taken as requiring a person to gather more information than it could have been expected to obtain in the course of ordinary commercial due diligence on a transaction of that nature.

Enquiry and notification requirements

251. A taxpayer can only be expected to provide the tax administration with information that is within that person's knowledge, possession or control. Information that is within a person's control includes information held by agents and controlled entities. As is the case for domestic schemes, mandatory disclosure should not require any person to provide information that is subject to a non-disclosure or confidentiality obligation owed to a third party.

252. Where a taxpayer enters into a transaction with a group member that has a material tax impact, then that taxpayer can be expected, at the time that arrangement is entered into, to make reasonable enquiries of those group members as to whether that transaction is part of an arrangement that includes, or will include, a cross-border outcome. In certain cases information about the scheme may be subject to confidentiality or other restrictions that prevent it from being made available to the reporting taxpayer. In these cases, where group members are unable or unwilling to provide this information within a reasonable period of time then the taxpayer should notify the tax administration of the fact that:

- It has entered into an intra-group transaction with a material tax impact.
- After making reasonable enquiries, has been unable to obtain information on whether the transaction is part of an arrangement that incorporates a cross-border outcome.

The notification should include any relevant information the domestic taxpayer has on the intra-group transaction and circumstances giving rise to the transaction. Tax administrations would be able to use this information as the basis for an information request under their existing exchange agreements with other jurisdictions (for example under a double tax treaty which contains an information exchange provision; the multilateral convention on mutual administrative assistance or a tax information exchange agreement).

Disclosure obligation on material adviser and/or taxpayer

253. As for domestic schemes, countries should choose whether the disclosure obligation for international schemes should be imposed on either the taxpayer or the promoter or both. When defining the disclosure obligations on the promoter, these should capture any person who is a material advisor in relation to that taxpayer or an intermediary in relation to any domestic transaction that forms part of that arrangement. As is the case for domestic disclosure rules, it will be important, when defining the scope of an adviser or intermediary, to ensure that the definition captures those who can reasonably be expected to have knowledge of the tax consequences of the arrangement but excludes those advisers or intermediaries who would either be unaware of the cross-border outcome or of the domestic transactions that trigger the operation of the mandatory disclosure rules in the reporting jurisdiction.

Information required

254. The information that should be required to be disclosed in respect of international tax schemes will be similar to the information required for domestic schemes. Such information should include information about the arrangement so far as it is relevant to the tax impacts in the reporting jurisdiction and should include key provisions of foreign law that are relevant to the cross-border outcome.

255. As part of the work on monitoring the outputs from the BEPS project, countries may consider whether the information required for international schemes could be standardised, in order to minimise the compliance costs that may arise from overlapping disclosure obligations imposed by different jurisdictions in respect of the same scheme.

Example – intra-group imported mismatch arrangement

256. The following example, which is adapted from the facts described in Example 8.2 in the Report on *Neutralising the Effects of Hybrid Mismatch Arrangements* (Hybrids Report, OECD, 2015), illustrates how the recommendations on the disclosure of international tax schemes might apply to an imported mismatch arrangement.

257. In this example E Co, a company that is tax resident in Country E, is an operating subsidiary of the ABCDE Group. E Co manufactures industrial equipment for sale to third party customers. The transactions E Co has with other group members primarily involve E Co making payments for intra-group services. The group structure is illustrated in Figure 3.1.

Figure 3.1. **Intra-group imported mismatch arrangement**

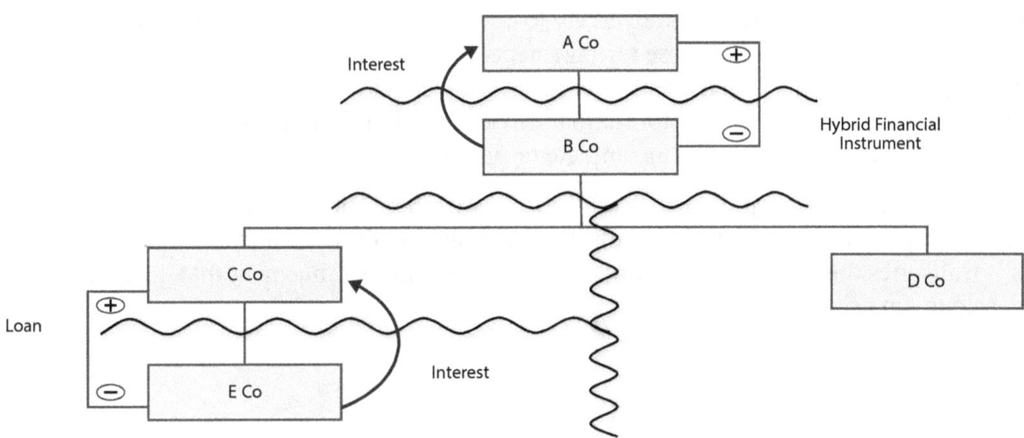

258. A Co, a company that is tax resident in Country A, is the parent of the group. A Co owns all the shares in B Co, a holding company tax resident in Country B. B Co owns all the shares in both C Co and D Co which are tax resident in Country C and D respectively. E Co is a wholly-owned subsidiary of C Co.

259. B Co is responsible for managing the group's financing operations and regularly borrows money from, and makes loans to, other group members. As part of these financing operations B Co borrows money from A Co under a hybrid financial instrument. Because payments of interest on the hybrid financing instrument are deductible by B Co but not included in ordinary income under Country A law, this is a deduction/no inclusion (D/NI outcome). E Co is recapitalised by C Co with additional debt funding at, or around the same time that B Co borrows money from A Co under the hybrid financial instrument.

260. Country E has implemented the recommendations regarding the mandatory disclosure of international tax schemes. A D/NI outcome under a hybrid financial instrument is one of the cross-border outcomes that is required to be disclosed under Country E's mandatory disclosure regime. It is expected that E Co will also have introduced the recommendations set out in the Hybrids Report (OECD, 2015) including those on imported mismatch arrangements. The imported mismatch rule will neutralise the effect of any D/NI outcome arising from a hybrid mismatch arrangement that is imported into Country E through the

interest payments on the loan to C Co. However, as noted further below, Country E may have an interest in ensuring the imported mismatch rule is being applied correctly and in monitoring the effectiveness of the hybrid mismatch rules in addressing the indirect risk posed to Country E's tax base by such arrangements.

Question

261. Is the financing arrangement entered into between A Co and B Co a reportable scheme under Country E law? What reporting obligations should be imposed on E Co given that it is not a direct party to any hybrid mismatch arrangement?

Answer

262. If E Co's interest payments under the intra-group loan are deductible under Country E law, and the amount of those deductions are material for tax purposes, then E Co will be obliged to make reasonable enquiries as to the wider arrangement that gave rise to the recapitalisation and whether those arrangements include a cross-border outcome. E Co will be obliged to notify its own tax authority in accordance with the mandatory disclosure rules of Country E in the event the information provided by other group members in response to any such request is inadequate, incomplete or unreasonably delayed.

263. The information provided by the group members on the wider arrangement and cross-border outcome may trigger a disclosure obligation for E Co and any material advisor if it transpires that the recapitalisation is part of the same arrangement that gave rise to the hybrid mismatch.

Analysis

The D/NI outcome under the hybrid financial instrument is a cross-border outcome

264. The D/NI outcome that arises under a hybrid financial instrument is identified as a cross-border outcome under Country E's mandatory disclosure regime. It is not necessary for E Co to be a direct party to that D/NI outcome in order to trigger disclosure obligations under Country E law. In fact, in this case, if E Co had been a direct party to the hybrid financial instrument, then the mismatch in tax outcomes would have been neutralised under Country E's hybrid mismatch rules and there would not have been any cross-border outcome for E Co to report under the mandatory disclosure regime.

The cross-border outcome and the recapitalisation of E Co are likely to form part of a wider arrangement

265. C Co provides additional debt funding to E Co at, or around the same time, that B Co borrows money from A Co under the hybrid financial instrument. The facts of this example do not provide sufficient information to determine whether the recapitalisation of E Co was part of the same arrangement as the hybrid financial instrument, however, taking the broad definition of *arrangement* and the fact that both transactions were financing transactions which occurred within a similar time frame, it may be reasonable to infer, in the absence of evidence to the contrary, that both transactions were, in fact, part of the same arrangement.

Recapitalisation of E Co triggers reasonable enquiry and notification requirements

266. In certain cases a group member such as E Co will not be aware of the existence of the wider financing arrangement or that it includes a cross-border outcome. This is particularly the case in the context of operational subsidiaries like E Co, where the transactions with other group members primarily involve making (deductible) payments for intra-group services.

267. The mandatory disclosure rules in Country E impose reasonable enquiry and notification requirements on taxpayers that enter into transactions with group members where those transactions have a material impact, or are likely to have a material impact on the tax payable under Country E law. Accordingly, if the recapitalisation transaction results in material payments of deductible interest to a group member, then E Co will be under an obligation to make reasonable enquiries as to whether the recapitalisation is part of an arrangement that includes, or will include, a cross-border outcome. If the group members are unable or unwilling to provide this information within a reasonable period of time, then E Co will be required to notify the tax administration of its inability to obtain further information about the arrangements that gave rise to the refinancing.

Enquiry and notification requirements not triggered if interest payment is subject to full adjustment under imported mismatch rule

268. As discussed above, the hybrid mismatch rules include an imported mismatch rule that is designed to protect the integrity of the hybrid mismatch rule by preventing taxpayers from engineering an offshore hybrid mismatch (such as a D/NI outcome under a hybrid financial instrument) and then importing its effect into the domestic jurisdiction through a non-hybrid instrument such as an ordinary loan.

269. In this case the imported mismatch rule may operate to deny E Co a deduction for the full amount of interest paid on the loan. If this is the case the interest payments made to C Co will not have a material tax impact in Country E and accordingly E Co will not be under an obligation to make any further enquiries as to the arrangement that gave rise to the loan or make any disclosure under the mandatory disclosure rules in Country E. As discussed in further detail in the Hybrids Report, there may be a number of reasons, however, why the interest payment to C Co is not subject to full adjustment under the imported mismatch rule. Such reasons include:

- The hybrid financial instrument is entered into as part of a structured arrangement involving a taxpayer in another jurisdiction and the mismatch in tax outcomes is fully neutralised by the adjustment made under the imported mismatch rule in that jurisdiction.
- Country C has also implemented the hybrid mismatch rules so that no imported mismatch arises on the facts of this case.
- The amount of the interest expense incurred by E Co under the loan is in excess of the deduction under the hybrid financial instrument or the taxable payments made by C Co to B Co.

270. In each of these cases, Country E has an interest in ensuring the imported mismatch rule is being applied correctly and in monitoring the effectiveness of these rules in addressing the indirect risk posed to Country E's tax base by such arrangements. Accordingly the disclosure rule will continue to apply in circumstances where, after the operation of the imported mismatch rule, the amount of deductible interest paid by E Co to C Co is in excess of the materiality thresholds set by Country E law.

Disclosure only required where E Co could reasonably be expected to be aware of the arrangement and cross-border outcome

271. Country E's mandatory disclosure regime will only apply where E Co could reasonably have been expected to be aware of the cross-border outcome under the financing arrangement. A person can reasonably be expected to be aware of an arrangement where the person has sufficient information about the arrangement to understand its basic design and to appreciate its overall tax effects. The information that triggers an obligation to disclose will include any information obtained by E Co through the reasonable enquiries described above.

Disclosure obligation on material advisor and/or taxpayer

272. As for domestic tax schemes, disclosure will be required from E Co's material advisors and/or the taxpayer (E Co) in respect of the recapitalisation

Information required to be disclosed

273. E Co and its advisers should be required to disclose information about the arrangement and the cross-border outcome (including key provisions of foreign law relevant to that outcome) and the direct or indirect tax impact of the arrangement and cross-border outcome on E Co's tax position. In the context of an imported mismatch arrangement this will include the calculation of any adjustment required under the imported mismatch rule.

274. In order to avoid unnecessary compliance costs, a taxpayer should not be required to duplicate the disclosure of information that is already fully and fairly disclosed under another domestic reporting obligation. For example, mandatory disclosure rules should allow a taxpayer to incorporate, by reference, information on advanced pricing agreements and other tax related rulings that has already been provided or made available to a country under Action 13.

275. In certain cases material information about the arrangement may be held offshore and may be subject to confidentiality or other restrictions that prevent it from being made available to the person required to make disclosure. In these cases the person making the disclosure should certify to the tax administration, as part of the disclosure requirements, that a request for such information has been made to the appropriate party.

Bibliography

OECD (2015), *Neutralising the Effects of Hybrid Mismatch Arrangements, Action 2 – 2015 Final Report*, OECD/G20 Base Erosion and Profit Shifting Project, OECD Publishing, Paris, http://dx.doi.org/10.1787/9789264241138-en.

OECD (2013), *Action Plan on Base Erosion and Profit Shifting*, OECD Publishing, Paris, http://dx.doi.org/10.1787/9789264202719-en.

Chapter 4

Information sharing

Developments in information exchange

276. The OECD has a long history of fostering greater tax co-operation and exchange of information between tax administrations. A major breakthrough towards more tax transparency was accomplished in 2009 with information exchange upon request becoming the international standard. This was also the year when the restructured Global Forum on Exchange of Information and Transparency for Tax Purposes started to monitor the implementation of the standard through in-depth peer reviews. A further step change in international tax transparency took place in 2014 with the approval of the *Standard for Automatic Exchange of Financial Information in Tax Matters* (OECD, 2014).

277. The legal basis for information exchange will be provided by bilateral or multilateral agreements between jurisdictions, which will generally be based on models such as Article 26 of the *OECD Model Tax Convention on Income and on Capital* (OECD Model Tax Convention, OECD, 2010a) and the *Agreement on the Exchange of Information on Tax Matter* (OECD, 2002). *The Multilateral Convention on Mutual Administrative Assistance in Tax Matters, Amended by the 2010 Protocol* (Multilateral Convention, OECD, 2010b) provides an independent basis for exchange of information. This Multilateral Convention provides for all possible forms of administrative co-operation between States and contains strict rules on confidentiality and proper use of the information. As of 1 July 2015 87 jurisdictions participate in the Multilateral Convention,[1] including all G20 countries.

Transparency and information exchange under the Action Plan

278. The need for improved transparency and information exchange is recognised in the Action Plan. Globalisation has resulted in a move away from country-specific operating models towards global business models that involve integrated supply chains and the centralisation of core functions at a regional or global level. Just as these models give rise to BEPS risks they also make the job of a local tax administration harder. Countries recognise that efforts to tax such businesses in the appropriate jurisdictions and on the correct amounts of income and gains cannot succeed without international co-operation and collaboration.

279. A number of the transparency measures under the Action Plan include requirements related to information exchange. The transparency framework developed by the Forum on Harmful Tax Practices in the context of the work on Action 5 requires the compulsory spontaneous exchange of information in respect of rulings that could give rise to BEPS concerns in the absence of such exchange. The framework sets out a two-step process; in the first step some basic information on the ruling and to whom it relates would be provided to another tax authority in accordance with the governing legal instrument; in the second step the receiving tax authority could ask for further information if this was foreseeably relevant to the tax affairs of their taxpayer.

280. The guidance on transfer pricing documentation issued under Action 13 also requires Multinational Enterprises (MNEs) to provide tax administrations with high-level global information on their global business operations and transfer pricing policies. The guidance sets out a three-tiered standardised approach to transfer pricing documentation. This standard consists of *(1)* a master file containing standardised information relevant for all MNE group members; *(2)* a local file referring specifically to material transactions of the local taxpayer; and *(3)* a country-by-country report containing certain information relating to the global allocation of the MNE group's income and taxes paid together with certain indicators of the location of economic activity within the MNE group. Guidance on the

implementation of transfer pricing documentation and country-by-country reporting is included in the consolidated report on Action 13 (OECD, 2015).

Expansion and reorganisation of the JITSIC Network under the FTA

281. Given the importance of improved transparency and international co-operation in combatting BEPS, and building on the progress in the area of information exchange, the Forum on Tax Administration (FTA) held the first meeting of the newly expanded Joint International Tax Shelter Information and Collaboration Network (JITSIC Network) in Paris on 4-5 March 2015.

282. The JITSIC Network is an international platform open on a voluntary basis to tax administrations and provides the opportunity to further enhance relationships to enable bi-lateral and multi-lateral co-operation and collaboration, based on existing legal instruments. Members of the JITSIC Network are actively encouraged to spontaneously exchange early information on emerging tax risks that may be foreseeably relevant to network members. This could include information obtained under a mandatory disclosure regime. Early exchange of information is not only important in addressing the revenue risks raised by cross-border aggressive tax planning but is also seen as a catalyst for closer and increased co-operation and collaboration.

283. The JITSIC Network offers a number of advantages over the more traditional forms of bilateral co-operation.

Active commitment to sharing information

284. Membership of the JITSIC Network entails an active commitment to increased sharing of intelligence, the spontaneous exchange of foreseeably relevant information and a focus on multi-lateral information exchanges. The JITSIC Network also provides an opportunity for tax administrations to aggregate the experience, resources and expertise of a number of different tax administrations to tackle issues of common concern.

Appointment of a SPOC

285. When a country joins the JITSIC Network it appoints a Single Point of Contact (SPOC) as a primary point of contact for network activities. The SPOC will not necessarily participate directly in any JITSIC projects but is the person appointed by the tax administration to manage the tax administration's participation in the Network. Having a SPOC as the main contact for JITSIC related projects facilitates interactions and the information exchange process and means that there is at least one person in each tax administration with responsibility for managing and monitoring the frequency and quality of that country's JITSIC interactions.

Establishment of best practices

286. The JITSIC Network provides an opportunity to test what types of information exchange practices are most effective and to promote these as best practices. Best practices can be used to enhance the quality of interactions under the Network and reduce the need for tax administrations to negotiate a framework for engaging with other countries each time they wish to collaborate on a project.

Secretariat support

287. The JITSIC Network is supported by the FTA Secretariat. The Secretariat does not actively participate in network interactions. Its role is to monitor the frequency and effectiveness of Network interactions and assist with information communication and capture. Secretariat support for the network includes the maintenance of a secure website and providing SPOCs with regular reports and updates on network activities. Sharing this information on a common platform increases the potential for interactions and multilateral collaboration and allows for information on best practices and emerging tax risks to be captured and shared with all the network members.

Exchange of information on aggressive tax planning and other BEPS risks

288. The JITSIC Network provides both a reliable platform for exchanging information obtained through the mandatory disclosure of international tax schemes and a forum for deeper co-operation and collaboration between tax administrations in respect of emerging issues that are identified as a consequence of such disclosure and exchange.

289. The JITSIC Network provides tax administrations with an efficient and reliable way to obtain further information about offshore structures that a tax administration considers may give rise to BEPS risks, such as those identified in Action 2 (Hybrid Mismatch Arrangements) and Action 6 (Treaty Abuse). It also provides opportunities for countries to collaborate with other JITSIC members to ensure that MNEs are taxed in the appropriate jurisdictions and on the correct amounts of income and gains.

Note

1. Jurisdictions Participating In The Convention On Mutual Administrative Assistance In Tax Matters: www.oecd.org/ctp/exchange-of-tax-information/Status_of_convention.pdf.

Bibliography

OECD (2015), *Transfer Pricing Documentation and Country-by-Country Reporting, Action 13 – 2015 Final Report*, OECD/G20 Base Erosion and Profit Shifting Project, OECD Publishing, Paris, http://dx.doi.org/10.1787/9789264241480-en.

OECD (2014), *Standard for Automatic Exchange of Financial Information in Tax Matters*, OECD Publishing, http://dx.doi.org/10.1787/9789264216525-en.

OECD (2010a), *OECD Model Tax Convention on Income and on Capital, Condensed version*, OECD Publishing, http://dx.doi.org/10.1787/mtc_cond-2010-en.

OECD (2010b), *The Multilateral Convention on Mutual Administrative Assistance in Tax Matters, Amended by the 2010 Protocol*, OECD Publishing, http://dx.doi.org/10.1787/9789264115606-en.

OECD (2002), *Agreement on the Exchange of Information on Tax Matters*, www.oecd.org/ctp/harmful/2082215.pdf.

Annex A

Further discussion on availability in the United Kingdom

For marketed schemes, disclosure under UK law is required when the promoter makes a scheme *available for implementation.*

A scheme is to be regarded as being "**made available for implementation**" at the point when all the elements necessary for implementation of the scheme are in place and a communication is made to a client suggesting the client might consider entering into transactions forming part of the scheme. It does not matter whether full details of the scheme are communicated at that time.

A person makes a scheme available for implementation if and when:

- the scheme is fully designed;
- it is capable of implementation in practice;
- a promoter communicates information about the scheme to potential clients suggesting that they consider entering into transactions forming part of the scheme.

The design of a scheme will typically consist of a number of elements (e.g. a partnership, a loan, partner's contributions, the purchase of assets, etc.) structured to deliver the expected tax advantage. The scheme will be capable of implementation in practice only when the elements of the design have been put into place 'on the ground'. So, for example, if the design includes a loan, it will be capable of implementation only if and when an actual loan provider is in place and funds made available.

Under the concept of *availability* a scheme can be regarded as being "made available for implementation" when the promoter communicates what is essentially a fully designed proposal to a client in sufficient detail that he could be expected to understand the expected tax advantage and decide whether or not to enter the scheme.

The "makes a scheme available for implementation" test was intended to trigger disclosure of a marketed scheme early in the marketing process. However, it became apparent that some promoters were taking steps to delay having to make a disclosure under the letter of the law in order to maximise potential avoidance opportunities before the tax authority was able to react to any disclosure. In the United Kingdom, the UK tax administration had examples of promoters taking steps to ensure that a disclosure was not triggered until virtually the point where it was implemented. As a result the application of the provision in practice was not consistent with the policy objective.

Consequently, the "**makes a firm approach/marketing contact**" test was introduced in the United Kingdom in order to ensure that disclosure of a marketed scheme is triggered as soon as a promoter takes steps to market the scheme to potential clients, as originally intended. It is the time when the promoter first makes a marketing contact: this intends to ensure that disclosure of a marketed scheme is triggered as soon as a promoter takes steps to market the scheme to potential clients. This test has to be considered before the "makes a scheme available for implementation" test.

Annex B

Compatibility between self-incrimination and mandatory disclosure

The information that a taxpayer is required to provide under a mandatory disclosure regime is generally no greater than the information that the tax administration could require under an investigation or audit into a tax return. Tax avoidance and tax planning transactions reported under existing mandatory disclosure regimes should not therefore give rise to any greater concern over self-incrimination than would arise under the exercise of other information collection powers.

Object and scope

Furthermore for many countries the types of transactions targeted for disclosure will not generally be the types of transactions that will give rise to criminal liabilities. Mandatory disclosure regimes are intended to obtain early information about aggressive (or potentially abusive) tax planning which often takes advantage of loopholes in the law or uses legal provisions for purposes for which they were not intended. Compared to tax avoidance, tax fraud (or tax evasion) has a different object and scope. Tax fraud involves the direct violation of tax law and may feature the deliberate concealment of the true state of a taxpayer's affairs in order to reduce tax liability. The cases of illegal tax fraud vary among countries but examples include false claims to exemption or deductions, unreported income, organised failure to withhold taxes, etc. which may result in a criminal charge.

Criminal proceeding

It is also understood that the issue of self-incrimination may arise if tax authorities require taxpayers to disclose some information about a potentially illegal scheme while criminal proceedings are pending. In such circumstances, tax authorities may wish to determine whether criminal proceedings have commenced or are under consideration at the time information disclosure is required.

However under mandatory disclosure regimes reportable information can be required to be disclosed prior to the actual implementation of a scheme. Such early reporting can be considered to be a part of the ordinary information collection activity undertaken for tax assessment purposes. To the extent that information is required merely for tax assessment purposes, taxpayers may not be able to invoke the privilege against self-incrimination at the time that disclosure of a tax avoidance scheme is required.

Disclosure obligation's compatibility with the privilege against self-incrimination

Mandatory disclosure should not, in general, infringe upon the privilege against self-incrimination. However, countries that impose criminal liabilities on taxpayers for undertaking certain tax avoidance transactions may choose to simply exclude those transactions from the scope of the disclosure regime without substantially curtailing the scope of the regime. In addition there should not be an issue with self-incrimination where a promoter is obliged to disclose instead of a taxpayer except in the circumstances where the promoter could have criminal liability in relation to the promotion or facilitation of a scheme.

In addition, if countries are concerned about the existence of some disclosable transactions which explicitly lead to criminal charges in any particular cases, countries can also specify that privilege against self-incrimination is a reasonable excuse for not reporting a disclosable transaction. For instance countries may consider a taxpayer to have a reasonable excuse for not disclosing a scheme where the scheme can be considered as a tax fraud subject to criminal charges.

Annex C

Interaction of penalty regimes and disclosure requirement

I. United Kingdom

Penalties which may be charged under the DOTAS regime are independent from penalties which may be charged when taxpayers make a statement on their tax return which leads to an understatement of tax.

Information about penalties for failing to comply with the DOTAS regime is published on the UK tax administration website.[1]

If a scheme falls into one of the categories where the user is obliged to disclose it under DOTAS rules, the user will be charged a penalty if they fail to disclose it without having a reasonable excuse. That penalty is entirely independent of whether or not the scheme works. Similarly, if the user of a DOTAS scheme fails to enter the Scheme Reference Number on their tax return, they will incur a penalty regardless of whether or not the scheme works.

Our Compliance Handbook contains information about penalties for inaccuracies, including inaccuracies in returns.[2]

Inaccuracy penalties are payable where the person's behaviour is either careless or deliberate and such penalties are based on the amount of tax understated, known as the potential lost revenue. It does not automatically follow that a taxpayer will be charged a penalty if they disclose that they have used an avoidance scheme which is subsequently found not to work. This is because penalties are not generally appropriate if the inaccuracy was made on the basis of a reasonably arguable view of the law that is not subsequently upheld.[3]

However, if the taxpayer is unable to show that they took reasonable care to ensure that a disclosed scheme was based on a reasonably arguable view of the law as applied to the facts of their case they may be charged a penalty. But that penalty is not intrinsically connected to the fact that they used a disclosed scheme. They would be in exactly the same position had they used a scheme which was not reportable under DOTAS and they had failed to exercise reasonable care.

A scheme may also cross the line into tax evasion if it requires a taxpayer to supply false information. Again, the taxpayer may be charged a penalty or potentially subjected to criminal action in that situation but that would be because they had taken fraudulent or dishonest steps to evade tax, not because they had used a reportable scheme.

II. United States

IRC section 6662 imposes a penalty on any underpayment, attributable to negligence or disregard of rules or regulations, substantial understatement of income tax, valuation misstatements relating to income tax, transactions lacking economic substance, and undisclosed foreign financial asset understatements, which may include underpayments attributable to tax shelters. For tax years ending after October 22, 2004, IRC section 6662A imposes an accuracy-related penalty on reportable transaction *understatements*. To be subject to the section 6662A penalty, the understatement must be attributable to a listed transaction (which is one category of reportable transactions) or to any other reportable transaction if a significant purpose of the other reportable transaction is the avoidance or evasion of federal income tax. The penalties under sections 6662 and 6662A cannot both be applied to the same portion of an underpayment (in other words, "stacking" of section 6662 and 6662A penalties is not permitted).

The IRC section 6662A penalty is 20% of the reportable transaction understatement where the reportable transaction was properly disclosed and 30% of the reportable transaction understatement where the transaction was not properly disclosed.

If taxpayers do not disclose a reportable transaction, they also can lose the ability to argue that they had reasonable cause for their tax treatment of the transaction (which otherwise would be one of their defences to having the penalty apply). The IRC section 6662A penalty, unlike the IRC section 6662 penalty, may apply even if a taxpayer has a loss for the taxable year, owes no tax, and has no underpayment.

The IRC section 6662A penalty also provides special co-ordination rules with other penalties that could arise from the reportable transaction. These rules generally result in application of only one penalty for the inaccurate reporting of tax.

Separately from penalties on inaccurate returns, IRC section 6707A imposes a penalty on the taxpayer for failure to disclose a reportable transaction. This penalty is not in lieu of any understatement or underpayment penalty.

Notes

1. www.hmrc.gov.uk/aiu/dotas-guidance.pdf – page 133 onwards (accessed 14 June 2015).
2. www.hmrc.gov.uk/manuals/chmanual/Index.htm (accessed 14 June 2015).
3. www.hmrc.gov.uk/manuals/chmanual/CH81130.htm (accessed 14 June 2015).

Annex D

Information power in the UK DOTAS regime

A tax administration may require additional information powers in order to enforce compliance with a mandatory disclosure regime.

Such additional information powers can allow tax authorities to:

- enquire about the reasons why a scheme has not been disclosed;
- require supplementary information or documents;
- require an introducer to provide information leading to the promoter of a scheme;
- request further information on an incomplete disclosure and the end user of an arrangement.

In order to use many of the powers described above, the UK tax administration must have reasonable grounds to suspect that a person has been non-compliant in relation to a particular scheme.

I. Explaining why a scheme has not been disclosed

The UK tax administration can require a person, suspected of being a promoter or introducer of a reportable scheme, to provide an explanation of why they think that a scheme is not notifiable.

Introducers are included within this information gathering power because it is not always obvious whether a person advertising a scheme to potential buyers is a promoter of that scheme or merely an introducer.

If the person to whom the notice is issued is an **introducer**, their reply should be that the scheme is not notifiable by them because they are not the promoter. The explanation should provide sufficient detail of their role in relation to the scheme to enable the UK tax administration to confirm that they are not a promoter. The explanation does not strictly need to identify the promoter in order to satisfy the person's obligation. If details of the promoter are not provided, then the UK tax administration have further powers to require disclosure of the person who provided them with information on the scheme as mentioned below.

If the person is a **promoter** of the scheme, they must, if required to do so, provide an explanation of why they consider the scheme is not reportable by them. In doing so it is insufficient for the reply to simply refer to the fact that a lawyer or other professional has given an opinion to that effect. Instead the promoter must engage with all the relevant legal tests.

In particular, where the promoter maintains that the arrangements do not fall within any of the existing hallmarks, the explanation must provide sufficient information for the UK tax administration to verify whether this is the case.

The information required at this preliminary stage is that which is required to test whether or not a scheme is reportable, not information that describes how the scheme works.

II. Requiring supplementary information or documents

The UK tax administration may require a person to provide specified information or documents in support of their stated reasons as to why a scheme is not reportable.

III. Requiring an introducer to provide information leading to the promoter of a scheme

Where the UK tax administration suspect a person of acting as an introducer for a notifiable scheme which has not been disclosed, it may require them to provide the name and address of any person who has provided them with information about that scheme. That person may be the promoter or another intermediary. This formal power will be used only if the introducer is not willing to identify the promoter voluntarily.

IV. Further information on incomplete disclosures

If the UK tax administration believes that a promoter has not provided all the prescribed information in relation to a disclosure, they may require the promoter to provide specified information and/or related documents.

V. Further information on the end user of a proposal or arrangement

If the UK tax administration suspects that a client on a client list is not a user of the proposal or arrangement but an intermediary, they can require the promoter to provide further information. The promoter is only required to provide the information it has in its possession at the time the written notice requiring the further information is received. The required information is:

- the name and address of any person on the client list who is likely to sell the arrangements to another person or achieve a tax advantage by implementing the arrangements;
- the unique taxpayer reference of that person;
- sufficient information to enable an officer of the UK tax administration to understand the way in which that person is involved in the arrangements.

Annex E

Comparison between different countries with mandatory disclosure rules

	United Kingdom	United States	Ireland	Portugal	Canada	South Africa
Scope	Income Tax, Corporation Tax, Capital Gains Tax, National Insurance Contributions, Stamp Duty Land Tax, Inheritance Tax (for Trust arrangements), Annual Tax on Enveloped Dwellings.	Income tax (individual, corporate), Estate and Gift tax, other federal tax	Income Tax, Corporation Tax, Capital Gains Tax, Capital Acquisitions Tax, Valued Added Tax (VAT), the Universal Social Charge, Stamp Duties and Excise Duties (but not Customs Duties)	Income tax (individual, corporate), VAT, immovable property tax, immovable property transfer tax, stamp duties	Income tax (individual, corporate)	Income tax, donations tax, Capital Gains Tax, VAT and any other tax under a tax Act administered by the Commissioner
Who Discloses	**Promoter** *or* **User** User must disclose where the scheme is devised in-house, the promoter is offshore or legal professional privilege applies. A "**promoter**" is defined as a person, in the course of a relevant business, who is responsible for the design, marketing, organisation or management of a scheme or who makes a scheme available for implementation by another person.	**Material advisor** *and* **Taxpayer** A "**material advisor**" is defined as any person who provides any material aid, assistance or advice with respect to organising, managing, promoting, selling, implementing, insuring, or carrying out any reportable transaction and who directly or indirectly derives gross income in excess of threshold amounts of USD 50 000 or USD 250 000 (or 10 000 or 25 000) depending on the type of taxpayer and type of reportable transaction. In addition, **taxpayer** is required to provide detailed information about the transaction and its expected tax benefits on a separate disclosure statement attached to the taxpayer's tax return, and the first time the transaction is disclosed to OTSA.	**Promoter** *or* **User** The general rule is that the promoter must disclose the scheme. User must disclose where the scheme is devised in-house, the promoter is located outside Ireland *and* there is no promoter in the State, or legal professional privilege applies. A "**promoter**" is defined to include any person, who, in the course of a relevant business, is responsible for the design, marketing, organisation or management of a scheme or who makes a scheme available for implementation by another person.	**Promoter** *or* **User** User must disclose where the scheme is devised in-house or the promoter is outside Portugal. A "**promoter**" is involved in designing, structuring, or implementing any tax planning scheme.	**Promoter (Advisor)** *and* **Taxpayer**[a] An "**advisor**" means a person who provides any contractual protection in respect of a transaction or series of transactions, or any assistance or advice with respect to creating, developing, planning, organising or implementing the transaction or series, to another person. A "**promoter**" means a person who *(a)* promotes or sells an arrangement that includes or relates to a transaction or series of transactions;*(b)* makes a statement or representation that a tax benefit could result from an arrangement in furtherance of the promoting or selling of the arrangement, or *(c)* accepts consideration in respect of an arrangement in paragraph (a) or (b).	**Promoter** *or* **User** The obligation to disclose scheme details is imposed on the promoter. If there is no promoter then the taxpayers must disclose the information. A "**promoter**" is defined as a person who is principally responsible for organising, designing, selling, financing or managing the reportable arrangement.

	United Kingdom	United States	Ireland	Portugal	Canada	South Africa
What is Disclosed	Arrangements falling within **certain descriptions** (known as Hallmarks) which are expected to provide a **tax advantage** as a **main benefit**. **Current Hallmarks** • **Three Generic hallmarks** to capture features indicative of avoidance i. confidentiality ii. premium fee iii. standardised tax product; • **Four specific hallmarks** to target known risks e.g. losses, leasing, employment income and Annual tax on Enveloped Dwellings. • There are separate descriptions to capture Stamp Duty Land Tax and Inheritance Tax schemes.	A "**reportable transaction**" is any transaction that falls within one of the following five categories: i. listed transactions ii. confidential transactions iii. transactions with contractual protection iv. loss transactions v. transactions of interest A "listed transaction" is a transaction that is the same or substantially similar to one that the IRS has determined to be a tax avoidance transaction and has been identified by notice, regulation, or other form of published guidance as a listed transaction. A "transaction of interest" is one that is the same as or substantially similar to a transaction the IRS identified in published guidance as a transaction of interest. These are transactions that the IRS would like additional information on in order to determine whether it has a tax avoidance purpose.	Arrangements falling within one of four classes of **specified descriptions** which are expected to provide a **tax advantage** as a **main benefit**. **Current specified descriptions** • **Three Generic hallmarks** to capture features indicative of avoidance i. confidentiality ii. premium fee iii. standardised tax product • **A specific class or classes of tax advantage** to target known risks e.g. losses, employment schemes.	Arrangements falling under this regime are involved with : • **One Generic hallmark** Transaction with a clause of waiving or limiting liability of promoter • **Specific hallmarks** i. participant of an entity subject to specially favourable tax regime or tax exempt ii. financial transactions giving rising to reclassification of the income e.g. leasing, hybrid instruments iii. The use of tax losses Disclosable arrangements aim at obtaining a **tax advantage solely or as its main purpose.**	A "reportable transaction" is an avoidance transaction that bears at least two of the following three hallmarks i. tax-results oriented fee such as a contingency fee, ii. confidential clause, iii. contractual protection Under the Canadian Income Tax Act, an avoidance transaction is a transaction that results in a tax benefit and **that cannot reasonably be considered to have been undertaken or arranged primarily for purposes other than to obtain the tax benefit.** The scope of reportable transaction has been broadened. The TS regime only includes gifting arrangements and the acquisition of property.	Reportable arrangements are classified into two groups namely '**specifically defined and listed categories**' and '**transactions with certain characteristics**' which are expected to provide tax benefits. • **Specifically defined categories listed by the Commissioner:** i. an arrangement that would have qualified as a 'hybrid equity instrument' if the prescribed period had been ten years; ii. an arrangement that would have qualified as a 'hybrid debt instrument' if the prescribed period had been ten years; or iii. *)* any arrangement that has been listed in a public notice • **Reportable arrangements with certain characteristics**: i. the calculation of any interest, finance costs, fees or other charges are wholly or partially dependent on the tax benefits derived by the arrangement;

	United Kingdom	United States	Ireland	Portugal	Canada	South Africa
What is Disclosed *(continued)*						ii. the transaction results in round tripping of funds, involving an accommodating or tax indifferent party or contains elements that have the effect of offsetting/cancelling each other or has substantially similar characteristics; iii. the transaction gives rise to an amount that is: a. a deduction for income tax purposes but not an expense for purposes of financial reporting standards; or b. revenue for purposes of financial reporting standards but not gross income for tax purposes. iv. the transaction does not result in a reasonable expectation of a pre-tax profit for any participant; v. the present value of the tax benefit exceeds the present value of the pre-tax profit derived by the participants

	United Kingdom	United States	Ireland	Portugal	Canada	South Africa
Disclosure of Schemes Details	**Users**: required to disclose the scheme by reporting a Scheme Reference Number (SRN) on a return. **Promoters**: required to disclose the scheme • Users are not, as a general rule, required to provide details of the scheme to the UK tax administration.	The obligation to disclose scheme details is imposed on both **taxpayers** and **material advisors**.	**Users**: Users are not, as a general rule, required to provide details of the scheme to the Irish Revenue. However, they may do under certain circumstances where the promoter does not (noted above). **Promoters**: required to disclose the scheme. (The general rule is that the promoter must disclose the scheme.)	**Users**: Users are not, as a general rule, required to provide details of the scheme to the Portuguese tax authority. However, they are required to report the scheme if the scheme is devised in-house or the promoters are based offshore. **Promoters**: required to disclose the scheme.	The obligation to disclose scheme details of a reportable transaction is imposed on taxpayers, advisors and promoters.	The obligation to disclose scheme details is imposed on the promoter and the participants. **Users**: Users are not, as a general rule, required to provide details of the scheme to SARS. However they are required to include the reportable transaction tax reference number in their annual tax returns. **Promoters**: required to disclose the scheme.
Process	• Promoter discloses scheme to the UK tax administration, usually within **five days** of scheme being made available to clients; • The UK tax administration issues a SRN to the Promoter; • Promoter must pass the SRN to clients who implement the scheme; • Promoter provides quarterly report to the UK tax administration of clients who have implemented the scheme. • Clients must report the SRN on a return affected by the use of the scheme.	• Material advisor is required to file a material advisor disclosure statement with the IRS Office of Tax Shelter Analysis (OTSA) by the last day of the month that follows the end of the calendar quarter in which the advisor became a material advisor; • Material advisor will receive a 9 digit reportable transaction number for the disclosed reportable transaction; • Material advisor must provide the number to all taxpayers to whom they provide material aid, assistance or advice; • Taxpayer must disclose by attaching a statement to the taxpayer's return and by filing the disclosure with OTSA the first time the taxpayer discloses.	• Promoter discloses a transaction within **five days** of the point at which a scheme is "fully designed" and a marketing contact is made, or within **five days** of making the scheme available for implementation by another person. • Where the disclosure obligation falls on the user, the disclosure must also be made within **five days** from the date of the first transaction entered into by the user, which forms part of the scheme. • The Irish Revenue must notify a unique transaction number to the person who disclosed the scheme. • If the scheme is disclos-able by a promoter, then the promoter must give that transaction number to clients.	• Promoter discloses scheme to the tax authorities within **20 days** following the end of the month in which the scheme was made available to clients; • Promoter does not have any obligation to provide the tax authorities with client lists who have implemented the scheme. • Users are required to report the scheme before the end of the month following the month of implementation if the disclosure obligation falls on them. (noted above) • No unique identification number system operates.	• A reportable transaction must be disclosed by 30 June of the following calendar year in which the transaction became a reportable transaction. • If more than one person is required to file a form in respect of a reportable transaction, filing of full and accurate disclosure by one of the persons in respect of the transaction satisfies the obligation of others. • Unlike the TS rules, there is no unique identification number issued for schemes.	• The reportable arrangement must be disclosed within 45 days after an amount has first been received by or accrued to a tax payer or is first paid or actually incurred by a tax payer. • SARS issues a reportable arrangement reference number. • Taxpayers must disclose that they entered into a reportable transaction and include the reportable transaction tax reference number in their annual tax return.

	United Kingdom	United States	Ireland	Portugal	Canada	South Africa
Process *(continued)*		• Taxpayer must include the reportable transaction number(s) in the disclosure statement if there is a material advisor and the material advisor received the number(s); • Material advisor must also maintain a list identifying each person with respect to whom the advisor acted as a material advisor; and • The list must be furnished to the IRS within 20 business days after the date of a written request by the IRS.	• Clients must include the transaction number on their returns. • A promoter is obliged to provide the Irish Revenue with a list of all the taxpayers to whom the scheme has been made available for implementation. However, Finance Act 2011 modified the original provisions by removing the disclosure obligation on promoters where they are satisfied that the client did not undertake the transaction at the time in question. If at a later time the transaction is undertaken, then the client details must be disclosed in the normal way. • The client list must be provided within a 30 day limit of the promoter first becoming aware of any transaction forming part of the reportable transaction having been implemented. • For "in house" schemes, disclosure must be made within 30 days from date of the first transaction entered into by the user.			

	United Kingdom	United States	Ireland	Portugal	Canada	South Africa
Enforcement	Failure to disclose doesn't affect the efficacy of scheme. [penalty regime] • Penalties for non-disclosure are up to GBP 1 million • Penalties if a user fails to report the use of a scheme on a return are GBP 100 for first failure, GBP 500 for second failure; GBP 1 000 for subsequent failures (apply to each scheme to which the failure relates). • Penalty for failure to provide a client list of up to GBP 5 000 per client omitted.	Failure to disclose doesn't affect the efficacy of scheme. [penalty regime] • Material advisor: The penalty for failure by a material advisor to disclose a reportable transaction other than a listed transaction, or for filing false or incomplete information with respect to such transaction, is USD 50 000. • The penalty imposed on a material advisor for failure to disclose listed transactions is the greater of USD 200 000 or 50% (increased to 75% in case of an intentional failure or false or incomplete filing) of the gross income derived from providing aid, assistance, or advice with respect to the listed transaction. • The penalty for failure by a material advisor to make the required list available to the IRS within 20 business days after the date of the written request of the IRS is USD 10 000 for each day of the failure after the expiration of the 20th business day, unless such failure was due to reasonable cause.	Failure to disclose doesn't affect the efficacy of scheme. [penalty regime] • Initial penalty for non-disclosures of up to EUR 500 per day is imposed during an initial period and followed by daily penalties of EUR 500. • The failure by a promoter to provide a client list attracts an initial penalty of up to EUR 4 000 followed by daily penalties of EUR 100, if the failure continues after the initial penalty has been imposed.	Failure to disclose doesn't affect the efficacy of scheme. [penalty regime] • Penalties for non-disclosure range from EUR 5 000 to EUR 100 000 for promoter and from EUR 500 to EUR 80 000 for user.	Any tax benefit from a reportable transaction is disallowed until properly disclosed (and applicable penalties paid), without having to establish that the scheme is abusive. [penalty regime] • Each person required to file is liable to pay a penalty equal to the total of all tax-result oriented fees and contractual protection fees to which promoters/advisors are entitled in respect of a reportable transaction. • Each promoter or advisor is jointly and severally liable with the taxpayer – liable only for the amount of fees that the promoter or advisor is entitled to receive. • Extension of normal reassessment period to no earlier than three years from date the form is filed.	Failure to disclose does not affect the efficacy of scheme. [penalty regime] • A monthly penalty for non-disclosure of ZAR 50 000 in the case of a participant and ZAR 100 000 in the case of a promoter (up to 12 months) is imposed and the penalty is doubled if the amount of anticipated tax benefit exceeds ZAR 5 million and tripled if the anticipated tax benefit exceeds ZAR 10 million.

	United Kingdom	United States	Ireland	Portugal	Canada	South Africa
Enforcement *(continued)*		• Taxpayer: The penalty for failure by a taxpayer to disclose a reportable transaction is 75% of the decrease in tax as a result of the transaction, subject to minimum and maximum penalties that range from USD 5 000 to USD 200 000 depending on the type of taxpayer and type of reportable transaction.				

Note: a. The obligation to disclose has been enhanced: under the tax shelter rules, only promoters are required to report the tax shelter to the CRA.

ORGANISATION FOR ECONOMIC CO-OPERATION AND DEVELOPMENT

The OECD is a unique forum where governments work together to address the economic, social and environmental challenges of globalisation. The OECD is also at the forefront of efforts to understand and to help governments respond to new developments and concerns, such as corporate governance, the information economy and the challenges of an ageing population. The Organisation provides a setting where governments can compare policy experiences, seek answers to common problems, identify good practice and work to co-ordinate domestic and international policies.

The OECD member countries are: Australia, Austria, Belgium, Canada, Chile, the Czech Republic, Denmark, Estonia, Finland, France, Germany, Greece, Hungary, Iceland, Ireland, Israel, Italy, Japan, Korea, Luxembourg, Mexico, the Netherlands, New Zealand, Norway, Poland, Portugal, the Slovak Republic, Slovenia, Spain, Sweden, Switzerland, Turkey, the United Kingdom and the United States. The European Union takes part in the work of the OECD.

OECD Publishing disseminates widely the results of the Organisation's statistics gathering and research on economic, social and environmental issues, as well as the conventions, guidelines and standards agreed by its members.

OECD PUBLISHING, 2, rue André-Pascal, 75775 PARIS CEDEX 16
(23 2015 37 1 P) ISBN 978-92-64-24137-4 – 2015-01

www.ingramcontent.com/pod-product-compliance
Lightning Source LLC
LaVergne TN
LVHW081417110826
845149LV00010B/1774

* 9 7 8 9 2 6 4 2 4 1 3 7 4 *